# Service Strategy

**FT** Prentice Hall

FINANCIAL TIMES

In an increasingly competitive world, we believe it's quality of thinking that will give you the edge – an idea that opens new doors, a technique that solves a problem, or an insight that simply makes sense of it all. The more you know, the smarter and faster you can go.

That's why we work with the best minds in business and finance to bring cutting-edge thinking and best learning practice to a global market.

Under a range of leading imprints, including *Financial Times Prentice Hall*, we create world-class print publications and electronic products bringing our readers knowledge, skills and understanding which can be applied whether studying or at work.

To find out more about our business publications, or tell us about the books you'd like to find, you can visit us at **www.pearsoned.co.uk**

**PEARSON**
Education

# Service Strategy

Management moves for customer results

Second Edition

Jacques Horovitz

PEARSON EDUCATION LIMITED

Edinburgh Gate
Harlow CM20 2JE
Tel: +44 (0)1279 623623
Fax: +44 (0)1279 431059
Website: www.pearsoned.co.uk

First published in Great Britain in 2000
This second edition published 2004
© Pearson Education Limited 2000, 2004

The right of Jacques Horovitz to be identified as Author of this Work has been asserted
by him in accordance with the Copyright, Designs and Patents Act 1988.

ISBN 0 273 67583 4

*British Library Cataloguing in Publication Data*
A CIP catalogue record for this book can be obtained from the British Library

*Library of Congress Cataloging-in-Publication Data*
Horovitz, Jacques, 1947–
    Service strategy: management moves for customer results / Jacques Horovitz—2nd ed.
        p. cm.
    Rev. ed. of: The seven secrets of service strategy. 2000.
    Includes Index.
    ISBN 0–273–67583–4 (alk. paper)
        1. Customer services—Management. 2. Consumer satisfaction. 3. Customer relations.
        I. Horovitz, Jacques, 1947– Seven secrets of service strategy. II. Title.

HF5415.5.H633 2004
658.8′12—dc22

2004046424

In some instances we have been unable to trace the owners of copyright material, and we
would appreciate any information that would enable us to do so.

10 9 8 7 6 5 4 3 2 1
08 07 06 05 04

Typeset in 9pt Stone Serif by 70
Printed and bound in Great Britain by Biddles Ltd, King's Lynn

*The Publisher's policy is to use paper manufactured from sustainable forests.*

# Contents

# Introduction

**I wrote** *Quality of Service* 15 years ago; the book became a success and was translated into 10 languages, probably because it was among the first published on the subject. In the United States as in Western Europe, companies were realizing that quality of product was not enough to provide differentiation. Japan in the 1970s and early 1980s had caught up with and surpassed the Western world in quality, requiring a fundamental change. Industry was shrinking while the service sector was expanding (and still is). Most of the work on quality and ideas in this area was geared to industry and production.

Over the last 15 years or so several things have happened.

Many, but not most, companies have realized they are not serving a market but customers. The personal computer industry and mobile telephone operators are beginning to appreciate this now because prices are declining and growth is slowing down – thus we have witnessed the multiplication of 'customer orientation' and ' customer satisfaction' programs.

In many sectors companies have gone a step further. Not only do they see themselves as serving customers rather than a market, they view retaining current customers as cheaper, easier and perhaps more profitable than attracting new ones. This was especially true of the early 1990s where growth in the Western world was minimal, thus reinforcing the need for customer orientation, service orientation, and customer satisfaction.

As a result, many books and articles have been published on this topic. Many gurus such as Tom Peters have emerged, and other offerings on excellence have been published that are almost religious in their fervour. Even the big six management consulting firms have started consulting on customer satisfaction. This would have seemed outrageous to them five or ten years ago, when most of their work was on efficiency, from the inside out!

So why another book on the topic, and why a revised edition after its publication in 2000 in English, German, Chinese, Spanish and French? There are
several reasons which, I hope, will entice the reader to proceed further.

- After 15 years, there are still many companies which pay only lip
  service to the concept of customer service. Only 30 percent of the
  Fortune 500 know whether their customers are satisfied. Only 10
  percent know whether increased satisfaction brings higher profits.
  There is still a need to evangelize!

- New sectors of the economy are developing an interest in the topic.
  They were indifferent to it 10 years ago. One could cite financial
  services, telecoms, and IT companies. Microsoft launched its first
  customer satisfaction survey in January 1999; public services and
  industry in general can be expected to follow. This book can help by
  providing an up-to-date systematic approach based on the work done
  with over 100 companies.

- As the Internet and e-commerce begin to grow, e-business will have to
  learn how to conduct a dialogue with customers without ever seeing
  them. This will require the use of innovative ideas to serve customers
  well. The technology will push conventional commerce to become even
  better at developing a service strategy, in order to stay competitive.

- Most books to date have been over-prescriptive. You read declarations
  such as 'Put your employees first' or 'Put your customers first.'
  Considering how progress is made by companies – often by trial and
  error – it is easier today to present a more contingent approach – i.e., to
  identify under which conditions and circumstances a particular
  approach will work best. For example, Chapter 1 deals with
  segmentation, Chapter 3 looks at different measurements and Chapter
  5 is devoted to loyalty. Each chapter discusses the conditions and
  circumstances governing what will work best, and will, I hope, help
  you define which route to take.

The reasons for this new edition after its publication as *Seven Secrets of Service
Strategy* in 2000 are therefore legion. First and foremost, the original version
was not in print but is still in high demand.

I have also tested the ideas several times over in the classroom with executives at IMD (International Institute for Management Development,
Lausanne, Switzerland) and realized that more details were required for it to
become a fully operational guide. I have also worked with both business-to-
consumer and business-to-business companies and realized that some issues
are different: I have tried to capture those differences in this edition.

The book is divided into seven chapters. Each represents one of the 'secrets' that I believe are the key to becoming a world-class player with respect to customer orientation, customer service, customer satisfaction and loyalty. In a nutshell they are the techniques I believe will gain a sustainable edge. In each chapter, I have tried to introduce a methodology: a step-by-step approach which you can easily use in your business. I have also tried to visualize the approach, so that it is easier to follow. Finally, drawing on personal experience of working with many companies in a number of sectors, I have outlined the 'don'ts' – observed mistakes made over and over again by many companies. Also outlined are the 'do's' – the questions one should ask in order to achieve a good self-diagnosis and get started.

This book is primarily designed for practicing senior managers and executives who think that a good service strategy is the best way to develop a sustainable competitive advantage. It represents the distillation of over 20 years of observation, interactions, real-life tests and pilots, and project work with many companies in different sectors. I have tried to be concise, giving examples to illustrate a concept, an approach or a tool. I have attempted to simplify as much as possible in the belief (verified experimentally) that what matters is not so much the complexity of the ideas you manipulate, but the systematic and intense execution of a simple approach.

Use this book as a reference guide for the systematic execution of your service strategy. And, please, in the era of the Internet, do not hesitate to give me feedback at *horovitz@imd.ch*.

Have a good read.

# Acknowledgments

First let me thank my family, Kathy, Tessa, Deborah and David. In order to spend time working on a book – and for that matter working on anything pertaining to customers – you need to feel well supported by your environment. This is why so many enlightened CEOs think that good service to customers will come from good care for their staff, and rightly so. It is even the title of a book: *The customer comes second and other secrets of exceptional service* (Rosenbluth and McFerrin Peters, First Quill Edition, 1992).

Second, let me thank IMD for giving me sabbatical space in early 2003 to concentrate on the book. Third, and this should be no surprise following the above, let me thank my customers. Over the last 20 years, I have had the pleasure of working in several countries, several industries, on smaller parts of big projects or as a facilitator or motivator on the topic of service as well as testing my ideas in the classroom with IMD participants. My clients were fantastic. They not only trusted me to help them improve their service, but let me test new approaches, and new ways of implementing them. Let me thank them one by one: 3M, Adecco, Andersen Consulting, AOL, Aquaboulevard, Banque Bruxelles Lambert, Banque Pictet, Banque Populaire, Banque Vontobel, BP, Boehringer Ingelheim, Boréalis, Bouygues Telecom, Carrefour, Carrier, Casino, Castorama, Caterpillar, Cebal, Ced Bursa, Celio, Ciba, Climat, Club Med, Cofinoga, Coloplast, Continental, Cowi, Credit Suisse, Danfoss, Disneyland® Resort Paris, Dow, DSM, Eliance, Elis, Essilor, First Leisure, FNAC, Fnac Services, Fortis, France Telecom, Galeries Lafayette, Generali, GrandOptical, GrandVision, Guidant, Häagen-Dazs, Haniel, Hempel, Hilton, Hippopotamus, Hopital Kremlin Bicetre, International Association of Department Stores, ING Bank, Initiative Media, Instruments SA, Lafarge, Lyonnaise des Eaux, Matra Telecom, Mercedes-Benz, Le Meridien, Microsoft, Midas, Mirabilandia, Mirapolis, M-real, Operator TDF, Orly Restauration, Otis, Peugeot, Philips, Pierre & Vacances,

Primagaz, Printemps, Productos Roche, Quick, Rabobank Renault, Rexel, Roche, Royal Canin, Scitex, Skandia, SNCF, Société Générale, Sorbus, Steigenberger Kurhaus, Stinnes, Tetra Pak, Texas Instruments, Valtur, Vision Express, Vivendi, Vodafone, Volvo, Xerox, Zurich Financial Services.

Finally, I would like to thank Estelle for typing and retyping my often difficult-to-read handwriting and Els, Research Associate, for helping my ideas become as clear as possible.

Lausanne
*April 2004*

# About the author

**Jacques Horovitz** is Professor of Service Strategy, Service Marketing and Service Management at IMD International in Lausanne, Switzerland. He focuses on how to compete through service and improve customer satisfaction, with heavy emphasis on service as a strategy for differentiation, on customer loyalty and on creating a service culture.

He brings to practicing managers three sets of experiences. First, he has *practiced* service marketing and management as Executive Vice President, Marketing and Sales for Club Med North America; as Managing Director – Marketing and International – for the GrandVision group, a listed retail specialty store chain with 800 stores in 15 countries in Europe; as coach to the Executive Committee of Disneyland Paris, during its turnaround, as well as Head of Quality and Training; and currently as CEO of a hotel chain he created seven years ago.

Second, he has *advised* the CEOs of over 100 companies throughout Europe on service, having founded, developed and managed a pan-European consulting company with offices in seven countries and 50 consultants. His assignments have been in a wide variety of sectors including leisure, tourism, transportation, financial services, industrial equipment, office automation, retailing, pharmaceuticals, automobile, hospitality, and telecom.

Finally, he has extensively *researched* service strategies and service quality, relationship marketing, and customer bonding, and published them.

Among his publications, his book *Quality of Service*, published by InterEditions in 1987, became a worldwide success: translated into English (1989), German (1989), Japanese (1989), American (1990), Spanish (1991), Finnish (1992), Portuguese (1992), Dutch (1993), Czech (1994), and Polish (1995). Another book, called the *Fifty Rules of Zero Defect Service*, was published by

First in 1989. In 1992, he published *Total Customer Satisfaction: Lessons from 50 European Companies with Top Quality Service* (London: Financial Times/Pitman), which has also been translated into German (1993), Spanish (1993), French (1994), American (1994), and Italian (1995). This book was reprinted in English by Pearson Education in 2002. In 2000, he published his latest book entitled *Seven Secrets of Service Strategy* (Financial Times Prentice Hall), which was translated into French (2001), Spanish (2001), German (2001), and Chinese (2002).

Professor Horovitz graduated from the Ecole Supérieure de Commerce de Paris, France, and has an MPhil and a PhD from the Graduate School of Business, Columbia University, New York. His academic awards include a Samuel Bronfman fellowship and the prize for the best research in general management from the American Academy of Management.

# 1

# Getting to know your customers: customer insight

**A service strategy starts** by looking at a company through its customers' eyes. But first you have to get to know the customers well. Who are they, what are their needs, what is of interest to them? What will motivate them to buy and buy again? What will make them satisfied, overwhelmed?

Then ask: 'Which customers?' Are you talking about the whole market? A particular subgroup? Do all customers want the same offer, or should the company have a special offer for some? Or would a common core offer, supplemented by specific add-ons for each subgroup, be preferable? And once your company has decided which target to go for, how do you make sure the prospective customers know the offer is for them? To answer these questions, this chapter will look at customer needs and expectations, segmentation, and targeting.

## Customer needs: from intuition to implicit and explicit needs

Discussing start-ups with entrepreneurs and observing entrepreneurial ventures, I have always been struck by the fact that companies are founded by people who have felt that the current offer did not meet the needs of customers. Take Nike, for instance. Nike was the brainchild of American university student Phil Knight, who liked to run, and athletic team coach Bill Bowerman. Its purpose: to provide quality running shoes at low prices, and replace Japanese imports.

In 1950 Club Med was created because Gerard Blitz perceived a need for convivial holidays for the French masses at the seaside. Dell was set up because, as a student, its founder Michael Dell felt a need for PC upgrades.

He saw that manufacturers were minimizing costs by providing standard models that did not have enough power. The founder of IKEA had the idea of making furniture immediately available in a market that failed to do so. Terence Conran's central idea for Habitat was to blend function and aesthetics at a reasonable price. And Amazon.com started because its founder, a heavy reader married to a writer, was tired of going to bookstores, not finding what he wanted there – not even advice – and finally having to queue. Original ideas and breakthroughs are not the fruits of intensive market research. Instead they come from a customer who feels misunderstood, inadequately helped, mishandled, and has enough drive to put a new idea into action. However, the key to turning that business idea and overall 'felt need' into a successful enterprise is a detailed understanding of customer wants. What will the idea do for the customer – provide new benefits, or reduce existing hassles? Figure 1.1 shows a detailed analysis of the Amazon.com concept, a bookstore on the Internet.

As the Amazon example shows, the Internet alternative offers many advantages. There are some limitations in terms of touching the product, receiving immediate gratification, or possibly testing (theoretically, you could read one chapter of every book in a shop, before buying). In every other respect, the web alternative is superior.

So consider:

- benefits (better performance, access, communication, reliability, support and help, advice, proactivity, experience, transparency);
- hassle reduction (less time, effort, energy, fears, uncertainties, doubt, costs).

Analyze needs in detail – once the need is experienced you have taken the first step toward understanding the customer better. However, needs are complex, and may be classified into two categories: implicit and explicit. Although they are critical, implicit needs often do not show up in market research. An engine, for example, is an essential requirement of a car. Yet for most customers it is not a very important factor in choosing a brand. However, if the car is unreliable, customers will become all too aware of it.

When you go to a hotel, hot water is essential – its presence is another implicit requirement. When you buy life insurance, it is implicit that your claim will be paid. The absence of such features will make customers extremely unhappy, yet their presence is so taken for granted that offering them will not predispose customers toward your company. Hence the disappointment of the design engineers when, in much market research, customers say nothing about 'implicit features needs.' That certainly does

| Customer steps | Comes to a store or site | Browses | Buys | Comes back |
|---|---|---|---|---|
| Benefits of a normal bookstore | Going out | Access to book, can read part of it, touch it | Discuss with other customers/advisor. Immediate gratification | Newsletter |
| New benefits through the net | Easy access 24 hours a day, 7 days a week | Largest selection, new authors' books | Recognition of who I am, mini-store for children | Regular e-mails according to the reading profile. Review of books by other customers, chat |
| Classical bookstore hassles | Parking, crowds | Time to find right book, not finding what you want, crowds | Queue to pay; not being attended; not knowing when order comes in | Not knowing what is cool/new |
| Hassle reduction | From home, any time | Multiple access for selection, book synopsis, bestsellers review | One click to fill order, notification of shipped order | Latest news customized to profile |

**Figure 1.1**  The Amazon concept

not mean that you in any way disregard such needs or adopt a sloppy attitude to them. Continue to improve them and maintain quality. But do not expect the work to have an immediate and positive effect on customers.

Implicit needs usually relate to the features of a product or service. Explicit needs are more concerned with the benefits (the engine is a feature; that the car runs is a benefit, which in turn includes other features) (see Figure 1.2).

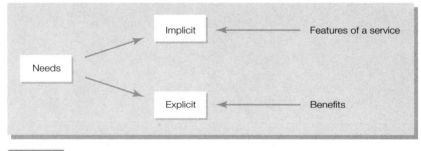

**Figure 1.2**   Implicit and explicit needs

# From needs to perceptions

In time, customers' needs turn into customer's perceptions (see Figure 1.3). Anything that influences those perceptions will have a positive or negative impact on customers' willingness to trust your company. These influences are termed 'filters.'

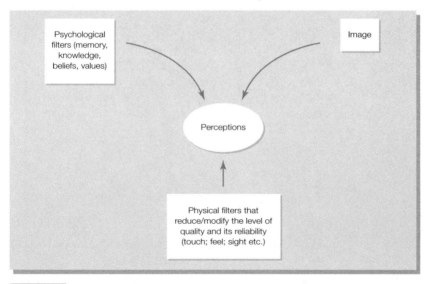

**Figure 1.3**   Factors affecting perception

## Physical filters

Whether physical or psychological, there will be elements in your offer that alter your customer's perception. A fish on a bed of ice seems fresher than a fish that is not. A clean desk in a consultant's office affects your perception of how organized that company's ideas are, and how reliable it is at maintaining confidentiality. Entertainment while you wait makes time seem to pass faster. So each time you appeal to the five senses to reinforce your offer, you strengthen a positive perception of its quality and capacity to fulfill needs. These 'physical clues' can lead a customer in another direction if you get it wrong. A dirty exterior in a restaurant speaks ill of its kitchen and cooking. A new tire on a car will not be perceived as such unless the wheel is clean. The use of glossy four-color brochures to state that your offer is cheap sends the wrong signals. If reception gives a name badge that fails to stay attached to a customer's jacket, it speaks unfavorably of your ability to deliver good service.

The physical filters I have described may either reinforce or destroy perceptions of the level of quality your company has put into service. There are other filters that can increase or reduce the perceived risk of doing business with your company – that is, the reliability of your product as well as its quality level. All studies on innovation show that customers have an aversion to taking risks. Few are prepared try something before others have taken the plunge. To get as many people as possible trying a new idea as quickly as possible, you need to address whatever makes customers perceive it as risky. It's called reducing the FUDs (Fears, Uncertainty and Doubts) of the customer.

When GrandOptical, a retailer that provides spectacles within one hour, designed its first shop, it chose white as the color and aluminum as the material. The objective was to reinforce the medical image, because of the perception among many customers that getting glasses in an hour could mean poor quality. And the word 'plastic' is not used to describe lenses; customers are asked whether they prefer 'organic' or 'mineral' lenses. The words can make a big difference in reducing FUDs.

A proposal for user-friendly office automation or for a 'customer-oriented' insurance contract may use words that will reinforce or destroy the perception that your company is 'easy to do business with.' Ford has scored with a simple feature. Every Ford GT engine is signed by the engineers who worked on it – as if those people made the whole car just for you! Thus, words, colors, material sound, support, smell, and texture all contribute to modify perception of quality (level and variability).

## Psychological filters

Beyond those physical filters, there are psychological filters that will also modify the customer's perception. These include memory, knowledge, beliefs, and values. Here are some true stories.

'I thought I bought it here,' said the old man to Nordstrom, a US department store chain emphasizing customer service. 'It' was a car tire.

'Of course, sir, we'll take it back since it does not fit.' Nordstrom does not sell tires!

Here is a contrasting example.

'I'm sure I left my wallet on the airplane seat near me on my way to London. Could you check with the cleaning people?' said the customer.

'It's impossible. If you had left it there, the cleaning people would have given it to us,' came the airline's defiant reply, instead of 'We will look again.' (In fact, the wallet was later found in a taxi and handed in at a police station. The police called the customer, but the workings of his memory led him to the airline first.)

Memory may work in strange ways, but customers' belief systems have to be considered too.

'I am furious with your after-sales service. Three breakdowns in a row, same cause. The spare parts you buy from the Far East are bad quality.' (The customer believes that Far East products are inferior.)

'I don't believe that you did the job well because you were only there for 10 minutes.' (So the customer believes good work means attending to it for a long time.)

How should you react? The customer is always 'right,' of course. These perceptions are genuinely felt. Only by reminding customers (counteracting lack of memory), educating them (counteracting lack of knowledge), and changing their beliefs and values can you change their perceptions. So why take them on in a series of endless arguments? They are right.

## Image

The third factor that affects perceptions is your company or product's own image. How you position yourself naturally influences customers. Image is built around a character, a personality and values, signified by the brand and dispersed through communication. Communication can be unintended as well as deliberate: consider word of mouth and rumors. Club Med in the USA has been plagued by the 'swinging singles, sea, sex and sun' image. At one point in the 1980s, a vigorous marketing campaign attempted to overcome this stereotype in a conservative market – anticipating perhaps the puritan mindset that greeted the Clinton/Lewinsky furor. But as recently as 1999, the *Chicago Tribune* reaffirmed the image, recounting how Club Med was obliged once more to focus on children in its American advertising. In the UK, the company's growth has been limited by another negative image: lack of comfort. This is an impression fostered by the earlier Club Med customers, who found that their accommodation consisted of straw hut villages. On the positive side, a successful campaign by Burger King (the 'true' hamburger) saw it regain market share in the USA. Thus, controlling your image as much as possible by communication (public relations, advertising) can do a lot to change perceptions over time. Also, make sure that early adopters or non-tryers get a better feel for the change in a brand.

Image building is a result of communication over time that brings clarity to customers as to what the brand stands for (either what it does for the customer, or who it is for, or what values it defends). However, for a service, there is an additional role that formal communication such as advertising must play: to make the intangible tangible. The challenge is to illustrate unequivocally for the customer what he could get for something which is intangible at first sight. And the more multi-faceted the service is, the more difficult it is.

Successful advertising/PR can make the intangible tangible. Look at Virgin Atlantic – the name itself plus the consumerist attitude of its CEO, plus its PR events made it the brand for those who are sick of giving their money to the establishment (i.e. British Airways) only to be mistreated. In addition, by introducing innovations (first to have movies on board, first to have beds, first to have 'eat on the ground, sleep on the flight') Virgin makes tangible the fact that its service stands for innovation and care for those who are disappointed by the establishment. To quote another example, Singapore Airlines since its inception in 1974 has always used the same advertising format: the Singapore flight attendant wearing local dress. This is a great way to make the warm, friendly on-board service tangible: The Singapore girl pictures are taken at home, in foreign cities, in a new plane, all of it to show new routes, new planes, tranquility and caring and warm behavior as well as exotic food. A great service ad!

# From needs to perceptions to expectations

Needs (unmet and met, implicit, explicit) are modified by perceptions, which in turn modify our expectations (Figure 1.4). Perceptions modify an 'objective' evaluation of how a service may answer a need. They introduce a subjective element into the judgment. Thus, the customer will not see whatever your company says or does in exactly the same way you do.

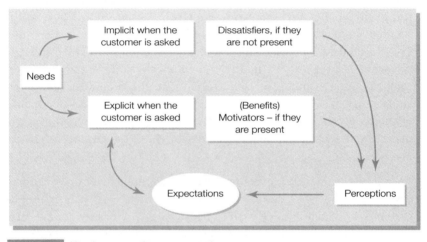

**Figure 1.4**  Needs, perceptions, expectations

Expectations, on the other hand, have more to do with the level of service customers perceive to be due to them, given their needs and perceptions of the offer. Say an airline loses my baggage on a transatlantic flight. When I land, my expectation is that the carrier will check thoroughly at the landing airport. The airline should tell me what the position is; I should not have to explain the situation to them. They tell me before I ask. I should simply have to give my name, baggage tag and declare the baggage's value for the airline to complete the paperwork. I shouldn't have to answer a barrage of questions. I should receive an explanation of what happened on the spot, and be given a short-term solution – that is, get my baggage or a phone call within 24 hours. If it is lost, the airline should compensate me to the declared value within 48 hours.

I have yet to find an airline that does this. On a trip to Chicago from Geneva via Paris, my suitcase was lost. Not only did I have to wait to establish that the baggage was lost, the airline refused to carry out a check beyond the baggage area. Then there was an additional delay while I explained what had happened, filled in the papers, and watched an official work on the computer using two fingers for typing. There was no short-term solution, no evaluation of potential loss, and no call next day. I called but hung up after 10 minutes of listening to music.

What created my high expectations in the first place? There were three reasons:

■ On a previous occasion another airline had found my baggage in the airport within 10 minutes. Since the baggage tag has a bar code, I knew from other industries that bar codes are used for tracking (for example, at Federal Express all shipments are tracked four times). So after a nine-hour flight, the information system should already have recorded something.

■ I traveled with someone else on the same flight coming from the same place. My baggage did not arrive, but hers did. I was also angry because I had paid an outrageous price (10 times more than the others who were on a group rate) to fly on the same airplane.

■ Finally, it was the carrier that sold me the idea of the hub from Geneva to Paris to fly transatlantic rather than going through Zurich.

In fact this example describes exactly how expectations are formed, and is illustrated in Figure 1.5.

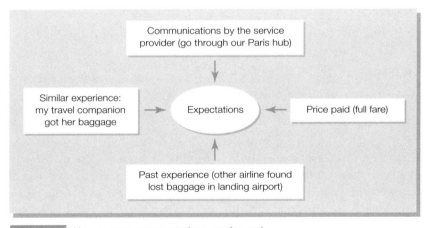

**Figure 1.5**  How customer expectations are formed

My expectations were formed not only by what happened to me the previous time, but also by experiences in analogous situations. Also, the more I pay, the more I expect. Finally, a promise of a smooth ride through the hub raised my expectations! So knowing the mindset of the customer, past experiences, and similar experiences will help a lot in understanding expectations. Narrow-minded companies – especially in business-to-business – carry out benchmarks on customer satisfaction by asking the customers to rate their satisfaction with performance by comparing it with the competition. Rarely have I seen studies asking the customers what their benchmark was in arriving at such an evaluation. It could be a supplier of other services; it could be their last experience!

# How to manage perceptions and expectations

Since all these items described above are linked, it is obvious that the best companies manage the whole chain by:

- Listing which needs are implicit – i.e., those whose absence will cause dissatisfaction, even if only explicit needs will actively motivate customers to use your company.
- Identifying how needs are modified in perception.
- Determining how expectations are formed.

This is especially important in the service sector. If this is what your business does, unlike product-oriented companies you are selling two things:

1  *The service itself*, whether a hotel room, a maintenance contract, or advice.

2  *The 'ability' to serve*, which in many cases the customer has to believe you can deliver.

World-class companies use the following tools to manage both perceptions and expectations (Figure 1.6).

## Peripheral clues

Peripheral clues are those physical communication processes that will reinforce the demonstration of your ability to serve before the customer is served. When Otis checks an elevator, you see the signature of the repair operative in the elevator. At FedEx, in 99 percent of the cases, operators answer the phone before the first ring (which tells you, 'We are efficient!'). JC Decaux, a company which manages bus shelters and their advertising throughout Europe, has white trucks to show its ability to carry out a clean and efficient job. Elis, the European linen service company, asks its truck drivers, called the AS (*agents de service*), not only to pick up and deliver linen but also to maintain an immaculate truck. Clean linen comes from a clean truck. That's a fact – sorry, a perception of life!

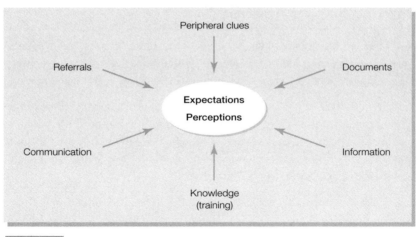

**Figure 1.6** Managing perceptions and expectations

## Information given to customers

Information can help customers to appreciate better or understand your prices. Amazon.com presents the review of critics as well as bestseller lists. Texas Instruments provides software that allows customers to compare its products with competing goods on the basis of total cost of ownership (TCO). This means that customers can use a number of factors – not just price – for comparison.

## Documentation

Both technical and commercial documentation should be clear, especially if you want to be perceived as transparent and user-friendly.

## Testimonials

Testimonials of customers help in reinforcing the 'ability to serve.' They have recently been used cleverly in Swissair's advertising.

## Advertising

In general, advertising should be aimed at under-promising so you can over-deliver.

Knowledge and training will go a long way to help customers understand better what you stand for. Those elements will help reduce 'false' perceptions or misplaced expectations, improving your company's chances of satisfying customers.

# Customer segmentation

Now that we have looked at what goes on in the minds of customers in general, let's narrow the focus and consider the differences that may exist between different groups of customers. To do this one uses a tool called segmentation.

Segmentation is a method of analyzing the complex reality of customer needs, perceptions and expectations by classifying customers into a limited number of 'homogeneous groups' – that is, people with similar needs or perceptions and/or expectations. It is a model of reality that helps companies make better, easier decisions.

Logically, for segmentation to be meaningful, the real-life situation modeled must be appropriate to the decision being made. Different types of decision require different types of segmentation. To illustrate this, here is a simple example: a car repair service. At the strategic level, the best market segmentation is one that separates the business into five categories.

- Work under guarantee (usually carried out by dealers).
- Work after guarantee (usually carried out by general-purpose garages or dealers).
- Specialty work (for example, body work, electrical work).
- Fast repair (generally carried out specialty franchise chains such as Speedy, Midas or Kwik-Fit).
- DIY carried out by people who buy spares and do the repairs themselves.

In each segment, the key determinants for success are different, as are the resources required. The key strategic decision is, 'Which business should I be in and how do I succeed.'

Suppose you decide to enter the fast repair business. The key decisions there are:

- how to attract customers;
- what will make them satisfied, and come back.

If you want to be an average performer, you will mostly use a segmentation that attracts as many types of customer as possible. The idea is that once customers come to one of your shops, fast service will be enough to satisfy them. If satisfied, they will come back and the loop will be closed. In this case, the best segmentation will mix criteria such as age of car, size of car, and density of cars in the surrounding neighborhoods. However, on closer examination, we will see that the criteria which help the company attract clients to the shop won't help it provide excellent service. In addition, a different model might also be needed for loyalty building.

Meanwhile, the best model for attracting customers could be one that segments by zone where people live or work (primary, secondary or tertiary, for ease of access). It would also segment by size of car (for pricing) and age of car (for products needed), and thus yield a segmentation that will help to decide on price, promotion, type of repairs and location of repair shops. Three segments would result:

1. Drivers in need: older cars, required by law, attracted by speed of service and sure to find the spare part that fits their old car.

2. The convenient: working or living nearby, attracted by speed of repair.

3. The competitive: this group has a choice between you and a normal garage; it is attracted by price.

These segments must be targeted separately by the marketing department, when deciding prices, promotion, product range and so on.

To ensure customer satisfaction, you should create a new model. Classifying or segmenting customers according to what satisfies them will group them under new headings. And the resulting segmentation will give you the means to do more than simply satisfy customers with a fast service. You will be in a position to 'delight' customers – that is, exceed their expectations. Let us assume that you have done your homework and developed two customer profiles.

1. *The car lover* Beyond changing the car's mufflers in 30 minutes, what will delight such a customer is a mechanic who talks about the car, shows what has been done, advises on other repairs, demonstrates new spare part packages, asks whether the customer wants to bring the old parts home (for transparency), cleans the wheels if the brakes have been changed, and puts a cover on the seat to protect it.

2. *The utilitarian* These customers on the other hand hate their cars. If you converse while they wait, talk about family, life and business. Don't explain what you do. Provide newspapers to read or send them to watch TV. Explain only the bill.

Now the car repair business has two models of reality: one for the marketing department, another for the operators in every station. There is nothing wrong with using different segmentations in one company.

Finally there is repeat business. Here you want to go beyond satisfying people and urge them to return. The best segmentation is that which rewards or recognizes two types of customer: those who come more often and those who have several cars. Yet another model of reality. In a nutshell, segmentation – that is, the recognition of differences between customers and similarities among a particular customer group – provides different results, depending on what you are looking for.

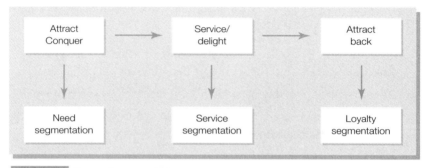

**Types of segmentation**

Figure 1.7 depicts three types of segmentation. Since the first type – need segmentation – is part of classical marketing, it is not covered in this volume. The second type, loyalty, is discussed in Chapter 6. That leaves the third type – service segmentation. It can be illustrated by a simple example: people eating or drinking at airport restaurants and bars. Marketers will come up with a set of segments to which products, price, promotion, and distribution can be adapted. These segments could include tourists (given guest menus, regular meals), business people, airport staff (who will be offered special prices), and groups (reached through tour operators). However, the customer service manager will recognize two entirely different segments: people who are in a hurry and people who are not. For the first category, the management will develop an express menu in the restaurant or will give the bill with coffee in a bar.

Another example involves people who buy toys. There are two segments: those who have children and those who want to bring a novel gift to a family with children (they respond to an invitation not with flowers or wine, but with a toy).

Again one sees different purposes and different segmentations. Managers usually fear two segmentations of the same market, but this concern is unnecessary. A marketing segmentation is used by those responsible for acquiring new customers. A service segmentation is for those who serve customers, and are unable to adapt to every individual need, but unwilling to treat all customers the same. The airport waiters, bar staff, and the heads of the restaurants and bars will use the second segmentation, whereas the marketers will use the first one. What's wrong with having different parts of the organization looking at their customers differently? The marketers' role is to get customers in, the service and operation people's role is to serve them, and again the marketers and sales people's role is to retain them.

# How to recognize who's who in service segmentation

The big issue for operations and service people is to match customers to segments correctly. There are three possible ways of doing this when you want to deliver a different type of service to different types of customers.

## Observation

To the mechanic in the garage, a clean car with no books, umbrella or maps on the floor suggests that the owner is probably a car lover. The bar staff in an airport coffee shop will note that a customer is in a hurry already has money in hand when ordering a coffee, or is looking at a watch, and present both bill and change promptly.

## Self-selection

In the same airport, the business person who selects the 'express menu' is probably in a rush and needs to be served accordingly. The customer who enters an FAO Schwartz toys store and immediately goes to the '20 toys selected' corner probably belongs to the group that doesn't have children and is responding to a family invitation with a toy in lieu of flowers or wine. Not knowing what to get, the customer is relieved and delighted that they had a 'store within the store.'

## Asking or probing

Would you like a sales assistant to explain the proposal, or would you prefer to read it on your own? Would you like a demonstration or not? Do you need help to start? In general, six questions can help identify between three to five service segments – sometimes more than you can deal with in your operations. When do you want it? How do you want it delivered? Would like me to take care of all paperwork? Do you want an overall bill or itemized?

Such questions will let you know very quickly whether you have in front of you a 'delegator' ('Do what you think is appropriate for my needs') or an order-giver ('I am in charge here!')

# Moving toward service segments of one

The last time I stayed with Ritz Carlton, in the mini-bar in my bedroom were at least six bottles of tomato juice. Why? On my previous visit, I had asked for tomato juice at the bar. Customer delight for the Ritz Carlton means knowing each customer's preferences in order to fulfill those preferences.

Peapod is an Internet supermarket. You can order your groceries for home delivery. Peapod wants to make your life easy not just by delivering the goods, but also by individualizing your repertoire, so you don't have to fill out the same list week after week. If you order baby staples once, the next time you order anything for your baby you will see on screen a list of the goods you ordered before, saving you the bother of typing the order again.

Levi-Strauss is now individualizing customer needs by producing made-to-measure jeans. Your measurements are taken once; the order is sent directly from the store to the factory and is back within 10 days. Your measurements are kept for the next time. Unless, of course, you change size.

When Robeco, an asset management firm, sends a mailshot to its customers proposing new investment products, its average mailing is only 4,000 letters. However, it gets a phenomenal 70 percent return. That is because it knows what each of the 4,000 customers needs, and can tailor its offers to them. This compares with an average return of 0.1– 2 percent for a normal mailing.

The UK supermarket chain, Tesco, runs a loyalty card scheme which awards one point every time you buy £1 of merchandise. You receive vouchers for offers in a category that appeals to you. Moreover, the vouchers are worth more if you buy Tesco's own brand. At Amazon.com you receive e-mails announcing new books, selected according to your reading preferences. All these firms and many more have moved to segments of one customer, employing various techniques to serve their customers individually. The best at this are dotcoms. Since they do not have direct access to customers they have put in place all the mechanisms possible to collect data about their needs and propose individual solutions. This is done at a relatively low cost, with data collated from past consumption, or simply by asking customers to give clues. Thus they are able to point out what you might like.

# Selling is a service: It is helping a customer buy!

This is not what all sales people have in mind when they push their product! Helping a customer buy requires an understanding of his or her needs and proposing the solution/or product that best fits those needs. Selling as a service goes beyond just good listening.

Take the simple example of an insurance product. There are two ways to sell it: either make a proposal that fits the risk to be covered or stay in regular contact to help the customer diagnose his current insurance contracts against all the potential risks he faces and spot inconsistencies. Within that diagnosis, you would then propose the specific new products. How many of us know exactly what we are insured against, at what level, and which serious loopholes we have in our coverage? How many of us are not even sure where our insurance contracts are?

Are insurance agents doing a good job by just responding to a specific request fast? Or would they do a better job by keeping a copy of all our contracts in their file, have a summary listing risks covered and uncovered, and update them with us once a year to reassess risks and changing conditions? This is service, and this could lead to more sales. Yet, although every insurance company sets an objective to increase their cross-selling (i.e. their number of products per client), every year when I ask where they stand, invariably they tell me around 1.4 per client. On the other hand, when I ask customers how many insurance contracts they have (from life to car to home, to travel to liability), they say around 10! The sales people sell products! They don't help the customer buy! Helping the customer buy means looking at all the areas suggested in Table 1.1.

**Table 1.1**    **Helping the customer buy: a few dimensions**

- Analysis of customer situation

- Help customer identify needs (sometimes not explicit)

- Reformulate needs in customer language

- Know about previous existing solutions to fill the needs, and how those solutions did well and did less well

- Help the customer make explicit his or her objectives or criteria for choice

- Help find a solution for previous existing solutions in the context of the customer situation (legacy issues, cancellation dates, etc.)

- Provide options and help the customer evaluate against criteria

- Make proposals customer friendly and easy to understand

- Help reduce the customer's fears, uncertainties and doubts by providing references, testimonials, etc.

- Help the customer find the right supplier even if it is not us

- Help their decision-making process: have enough copies of proposals in full and summary form (personalized for each decision maker), a table summarizing the different options including competitors and their scores on the criteria, etc.

- Provide a summary of the legal aspects to highlight what the customer should be aware of

- Send reminders when the proposal has deadlines so that the customer is always aware of them

- Prepare trade-off analysis in case some options do not yield the same results but have other advantages

- Give a personal recommendation when the customer can't make up their mind or when their choice seems to be inadequate for their needs

## Summary

A new customer need is not identified by analyzing feedback from satisfied customers. It will come from someone who, as a customer, felt badly served. But once the overall need is identified, understanding customers can suggest in great detail what they would like to see. Your customers do not evaluate how your company responds to their needs in an objective or neutral manner.

Some customer needs are implicit, and are not expressed by customers unless they are missed. Physical or psychological filters combined with image can modify customers' perceptions of the offer. Since perceptions are all that a customer can express, it is not the company's business to dispute them, even if they are objectively wrong, but to modify them. Expectations set the level of service that the customer has in mind. Expectations also need to be managed through pricing, documentation, advertising, information or education, rather than being disputed.

Segmentation, up to the point where segments of one can be achieved, allows a company to use the appropriate model to attract a particular group of customers, serve them well, and make them come back. Several segmentations can work in parallel within the same company, since different people within the company use them.

# Don'ts

**1** Don't rely on the customers to express needs. Test your intuition on them.

**2** Don't stop meeting the latest needs of customers just because they haven't shown up in the satisfaction surveys.

**3** Don't fight customers' perceptions or expectations: manage them.

**4** Don't say the customer is not always right. They are – from their standpoint.

**5** Don't model your own company after one segmentation.

# The 10 service segmentation questions

**1** What are your mechanisms for continuously sensing your target customers' potential and actual needs, expectations, remarks, suggestions?

**2** How many ideas did you get last year from listening to your customers?

**3** Do clients all want the same service?

**4** If not, what is common? What is different?

**5** Given the response to Question 3, is it possible to serve everyone the same way (same operation, same organization) or is it better to have a separate service (a shop within the shop)? A separate structure?

**6** What mechanism can be used to identify which customer belongs to which segment? Self-selection, observation, questions, or a mix?

**7** Are your service people sufficiently well trained to recognize who is who?

**8** How do you regularly monitor change in segmentation to anticipate or at least accompany change?

**9** Can you have the same segmentation for (a) conquest, (b) satisfaction (service quality), and (c) loyalty building – or do you need a separate one for each?

**10** What mechanism do you use for managing perceptions? Does it work? What mechanism do you use for managing expectations? Does it work?

# 2

# Creating customer value: the service concept

**In marketing circles**, there is much talk about service concepts that provide value to the customer. However, the term 'value' can have many different meanings. For some, it is a good deal for what you pay; for others, it is a service offer that brings either truly innovative benefits or benefits that outstrip what is currently available. In this chapter, I will look at the design and definition of value in the context of providing outstanding service. Since business-to-business service is different from business-to-consumers, I will look at the business-to-business value proposition separately. Once value is defined, what makes it truly successful is how a service provider translates the definition into day-to-day encounters with customers. This is what allows the value to be expressed and perceived. Finally, I will revisit the issue of communicating value to the customer.

## Value = benefits − costs: the benefit element of the equation

Customers receive value when the benefits from a product or service exceed what it costs to acquire and use it. That is the fundamental equation. The greater the difference between the two, the higher the value.

Let's look at the benefits first. A benefit is what the product does for me as a customer. A car for transport or a car to express my ego; an air filter to clean air; a drilling machine to make holes. Such are the benefits offered by products. Then there are services. Software to create a website; a hotel room to rest in; a resort for relaxation; insurance to protect my income, my assets or myself from my mistakes or those of others. A haircut for appearance; a theme park for family entertainment; an information or a training kit to help me use a machine, and advice to solve a problem.

If the benefits provided by your products are greater than or different to those offered by other companies, but cost the same, then you are offering better value. If one of those benefits conferred is significantly better than what others are able to provide at equal cost, then you offer superior value. For instance, Formule 1, launched by Accor in 1985, is a one-star hotel chain that targets traveling sales representatives and students. The benefits provided by budget hotels should include convenient location, cleanliness, 24-hour access, and safety. But Formule 1 also offers better hygiene, quietness and bed quality – benefits that you don't usually get in cheap hotels. It has outpaced the budget price hotel category, building 300 such hotels across Europe in 15 years. The Marriott Courtyard hotel – although in a different category – was developed on the same principles. Its mission is to offer superior benefits to the traveling businessperson by focusing on the room size (suite). Virgin Atlantic is another example of superior benefits, judged in terms of comfort (business class at the price of full economy fare), fun, and even ground transport (provided from home to airport on a motor-cycle when there's too much traffic to take a car).

There are several ways in which extra value can be provided through the benefit side of the equation.

## Focusing on attribute: benefit improvement

Focus on one or a small few of the product's attributes and improve one of the benefits offered beyond the current range (Figure 2.1). LensCrafters, for example, has 700 optical stores in the US. The company has concentrated relentlessly on its ability to offer prescription spectacles in *one hour* for the customer who goes to shopping malls and is pleased with one-stop shopping for glasses.

Wells Fargo has converted its bank branch network to accommodate super-market facilities, and invited drugstore chains to set up pharmacies in its existing branches. Consider the logic. To pay for purchases you need money, and to get money you go to a bank. Locating banking services closer to where customers spend their money is a good move. By focusing on one benefit – *location* – Wells Fargo has made banking more convenient to customers.

Another example is the metamorphosis of Atlanta Airport and Heathrow Airport, which followed what had happened much earlier in places like Singapore and Copenhagen. A dull, purely functional airport was turned

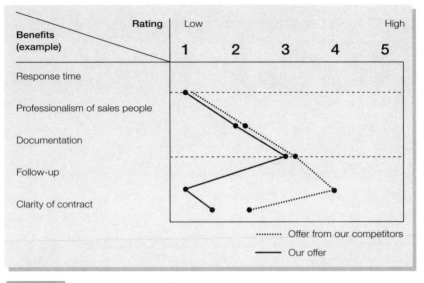

**Figure 2.1** Improving one benefit or feature

into an exciting complex, complete with user-friendly services and a shopping mall. After all, what customers must do in an airport is wait. It's tedious. They might as well *shop*.

## Extending benefits: creating solutions

Extend the benefits to auxiliary services that the customer may need when using your service. British Airways offers showers or trouser pressing to its Executive Club members after a long flight. The extended benefits here are to prepare the customer for the next meeting. Federal Express offers businesses the ability to place, track and bill their own FedEx orders inhouse. Through FedEx Powership® at *www.fedex.com*, customers can schedule pick-ups, track orders and have deliveries confirmed. The extended benefits are self-regulation of pace, immediate information and reassurance. In both examples, the extra services provided have pushed the service concept before, after or during use of the service by the customer.

One way to think about extension is to look at the customer activities. It allows us to think of those additional longitudinal benefits (Figure 2.2).

If you buy production equipment, it is to manufacture certain products at a certain price for use by certain customers. Beyond selling the machine, what else can the equipment suppliers add to their offer? There could be preventive maintenance contracts, perhaps, to allow continuous use of the machine, or they could provide studies on their customers, to help sell the products manufactured by the machines.

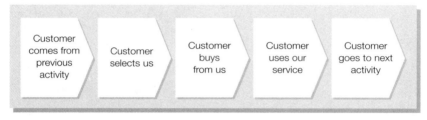

Figure 2.2 **Adding customer benefits**

If customers use an airline to go from point A to point B, customer-centered management will work out where they come from and what their destination is. Then the company can consider providing extended services. Do customers need transport from A to B? What shape must they be in? This approach applies to other businesses, too. An investment bank might consider extending its services to pre-acquisition analyses of management style, potential meshing of culture, and other analyses that are softer than pure numbers, as well as to post-acquisition exploitation of synergy.

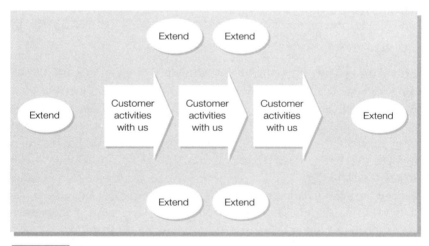

Figure 2.3 **Extending the value chain**

Thus opportunities for extending value exist before, after, and around the classical activities the customer engages in with your company (Figure 2.3). And by grasping these opportunities, you provide more than a service: you give a solution to the customer.

Zurich Financial Services transformed the way it undertakes its car insurance business by moving to provide a total care solution. Previously, when your car was involved in an accident, you had to get it to a repair shop. You had to call an expert, who would come to evaluate the damage and authorize the repair work. Then you had to supervise the job done at the repair shop and get your car back. These days you can leave your car at any Shell station. Within 30 minutes you get a replacement. The insurance company selects a repair shop, and arranges for your car to be taken there; it is repaired and returned to the Shell station nearest your home! No need to call an expert, no walking, no supervision of repairs; no haggling with the expert or the repair shop! And no loss of time. Value has been extending by providing extra benefits over a longer time and taking into account different needs in the aftermath of an accident.

In Europe, Kwik-Fit is the biggest independent chain of car repair and spare parts shops. There are 750 retail outlets in the UK and the Benelux countries. It has launched a one-stop shop for motor insurance. Associated with a seven-day telecenter, which has a local number, it offers a one-contact service for claims and repair. As an inducement, all policyholders get a freephone number to use as a safety measure in case of car accidents. Value extension is again provided by adding one-stop facilities, in this case shopping for car repair and insurance.

Many petrol stations in Europe have done likewise. Managers looked at people coming for fuel and considered where they came from (work), where they were going (home), and when they came (off-peak times by store norms, because of traffic). Apart from fuel, what did they need? Food, newspapers, bread, and other such provisions were the obvious purchases. But why buy at a petrol station? Because it's convenient (free, easy parking, on your way); and with most small grocery stores having disappeared, it is probably closest to home.

Very few city-center restaurants in Europe have understood that dining out means having to take the car into town. This is a hassle if there is no parking near the restaurant. Even then, people may be afraid to leave their cars unattended. Having someone look after this for you is an extra benefit. It extends value; it is good business.

General Motors Saturn car dealers in Florida went further in extending the benefits of car repair. The company has invented the docking station, which consists of a factory-trained technician driving a customized service van. This service department on wheels lets the technician perform routine maintenance and light repairs such as oil changes and engine tuning in a home driveway or an employee parking lot. The van, its tools and laptop computer for information and credit card processing are valued at $100,000. Customers pay only a $5.00 surcharge. Each service takes 45 minutes, so that one van can complete 10–15 service calls per day. Chrysler has the same concept. Who says the customer has to go to a garage?

To extend value in this way, you do not have to provide instantaneous benefits – i.e., benefits enjoyed while the service is being delivered. Chrysler has devised computer software that, when installed on the customer's computer, will display a service reminder when vehicles are due for scheduled maintenance. Chrysler had 37,000 copies of this software distributed through dealers in 1997, and 40 percent of the customers came back to their dealers within six months of receiving the program.

Pioneer Hi-Bred International, Inc., a DuPont company, is the world's leading developer and supplier of advanced plant genetics to farmers worldwide. But it has increased its success not just by selling seeds but also by providing information on seed productivity, farm management and the like. The customer experiences this extension of value before using the seeds.

Otis repairs elevators. Knowing that building managers consider a number of factors when choosing a repair company, Otis includes in its service package information on breakdowns and their duration. When owners or renters query the costs of elevator maintenance, or ask why the elevator seems to break down so often, managers can give answers. This added value serves to reassure customers about their choice of contract, and takes place after use of the service.

## Beyond solutions: an experience

The third way to create value through additional benefits is to go from a solution to a positive 'experience': that is, to add intangibles to the tangible and to add soft aspects to service. Club Med has long been at the forefront of such a value expansion in creating the club 'experience.'

- It is not a resort or a hotel, but a village, and it is built like a village with its centre, theatre, and agora.
- It is not food. It is a display of the world's cuisine.
- It is not equipment. It is learning something new (sports, arts and crafts).
- It is not just doing something or nothing. It is meeting people.
- It is not a night show. It is continuous fun and celebration.

Fun is creeping into everything. Today there is talk of edutainment (as LEGO terms new educational toys), and 'retailtainment,' in which retailing and entertainment are mixed. The most famous example is the Caesars Palace shopping gallery in Las Vegas, where night and day alternate every 10 minutes, and the whole gallery looks like an ancient Roman street complete with costumed Romans. It claims the most sales per square meter in the world, welcoming 30 million visitors each year.

In the Toyota showroom in Tokyo, one floor is dedicated to each targeted customer group. There is a floor for professional women, another for couples, singles, families, and so on. As well as showing the appropriate cars, each floor has merchandise, orchestras, and other events customized for the group in question. The Mall of America in Minneapolis has in its centre a 32-acre theme park in addition to its hundreds of specialty shops, and four department stores.

What's true of retailing is true of the restaurant trade, too. Thus restaurants have been themed: Planet Hollywood, Rainforest Cafe, Conran's Alcazar in Paris, and so on. Supermarkets and hypermarkets have also started to theme the presentation of the merchandise to make buying food less of a chore. In the UK, Tesco sells milk in a farm-like setting. Creating an experience has gone further in specialty shops. The Walking Company in California is a store dedicated to the entire walking experience. When you enter the shop, the design of the walls and floors is calculated to make you feel as if you are already walking in the mountains. Airlines have also got on the bandwagon, with movies and games machines (Singapore Airlines) or hairdressers (Virgin).

The experiential dimension is not limited to retailing or tourism, however. In every business, there are elements that will improve the 'experience' a customer gets from using a supplier.

- Peripheral elements such as the bill: Is it easy to understand and to relate to what was bought?
- The relationship created: Everyone knows that in order for a merger to work, the top teams need to work together. Overly serious, number-crunching investment bankers tend to forget team-building exercises when they advise their clients on an acquisition or merger.
- The core element – use of a product. Is it easy for the customer to learn how to use the machine or the software? How user-friendly is the documentation or hotline?
- Even the business proposal can be a positive experience: 'It was pleasant to read, I got the feeling they understood me and wanted my business.'

■ Meeting the organization ('Each time I go there for a product demonstration or a joint R&D session, I feel I am part of the family'), etc.

In summary, there are three ways to increase value. They are as shown in Figure 2.4.

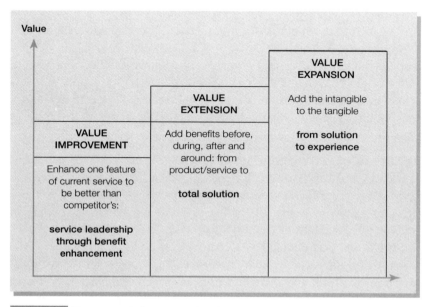

**Figure 2.4** Three ways to increase value through benefit improvement, extension or expansion

## The cost element of the value equation

Value is a comparative relationship between benefits and costs, and clearly the issue of costs can have a significant impact on the customer's perception of value.

We often think of cost as the monetary purchase (or sale) price of a product or a service. This is wrong. Cost, from the customer's point of view, has three elements:

■ Money paid.

■ Costs and effort of getting the product or service (understanding the contract, understanding the offer, finding the location, time to find a good salesperson).

■ Costs and effort of using the product or service properly (returning wrong shipments; bad quality; time taken to get the problems fixed; price of spare parts, inventory; disposal).

The monetary price is sometimes just a small part of the total cost of getting and using a product or service. The car industry exemplifies this. 25 percent of the cost to the customer is the machine itself; 10 percent is insurance; 35 percent is petrol and oil; and spares account for about 30 percent. The total cost of ownership of a car is certainly not based on its selling price! Texas Instruments presents the price of its electronic components to its customers:

*Total cost of ownership = purchasing cost + quality control cost + inventory cost + return cost + logistics costs. (Even if the purchaser cost is higher for Texas Instruments compared with a competitor, the total cost of ownership is lower.)*

In fact, many car manufacturers are now selling complete transport solutions, not just cars.

The costs are either in cash (maintenance expenses, for example) or the time and effort necessary to buy and use a product or service. In an age where time is at a premium and there are more opportunities than time available, consider also the opportunity costs. IBM has segmented its after-sales service market into four categories, with large manufacturing facilities constituting the top segment. A top segment customer is one for which the cost of computer downtime would be more than $100,000. For such customers, preventive maintenance, on-site presence and fast repair time are more important than the cost of the customer engineer or spare parts.

A salutary example of a product that imposes excessive, additional costs on the customer is the electronic cash card. It is typical of a service oriented not toward the customer but toward the supplier, in this case the bank. With electronic cash, a bank can reduce the cost of handling cash and providing local services such as cash and check deposits or lodgments to traders. But for the customer, the card means having to load a certain amount on the card (this means going to an ATM, a first 'cost'). When the money runs out, another cost is the fear of not being able to pay for a full purchase – stress is a cost! For the retailer there is yet another cost: card readers. Finally, with current methods – cash and credit cards – customers know they can choose to pay now or later. If there is no alternative to the cash card, we would have to pay on the spot (unless the chip was programmed to allow delayed payment).

This apparent lack of freedom gives the customer more aggravation. Unsurprisingly, these cards are not successful. Any service provider that makes customers waste their time is out of touch with the reality of the market-place, and eliminates the benefit the company may have created in the first place.

In the competition between insurance companies, to take another example, direct insurance sellers attempt to reduce the time and effort needed for the customer to sign up for auto insurance (orally, by phone) and cut the time required to fill the claim (by phone). Compared with traditional insurance, the cost to the customer is lower.

In summary, good value needs good benefits for the customer at favorable terms – taking into account both the financial and the non-financial costs incurred in buying and using the service.

# Reducing the price

Price is a key element in the cost incurred by customers. If a company can reduce its costs totally or partly by reinvesting the savings, to be able to give lower prices to the customers, while maintaining or even increasing the benefits, then value will increase. This strategy is called 'outpacing.'

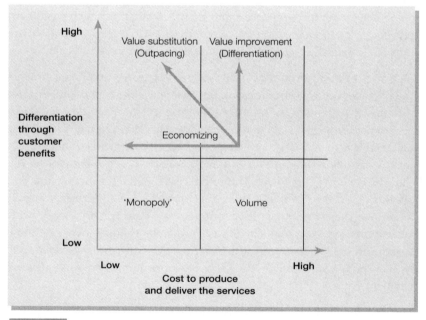

**Figure 2.5**  Elements of an outpacing strategy

Three strategies can be used to achieve the outpacing segment in Figure 2.5.

▪ Reduce cost and price without touching benefits: the strategy of economizing.

▪ Increase benefits and reduce costs at the same time: the strategy of value substitution.

▪ Increase benefits with the same cost structure: the strategy of improvement.

All three strategies have a common tool, value delivery chain analysis, but the use made of it is different. The value delivery chain is a model used to describe the components and activities necessary for a company to deliver a particular product or service. Figure 2.6 describes the value chain in the furniture industry. In the first strategy we see **economizing** – costs or prices or both could be reduced by relocating the production of parts to the Far East, where materials and labor are cheaper. This is what some manufacturers have done. Unfortunately a single-track, cost-reduction approach does not always permit benefits to be kept intact. Cheaper labor often seems less professional (especially in the services sector), which in turn leads to reduced service.

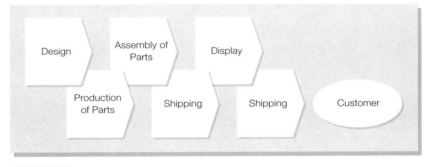

 **Value chain analysis**

In the second strategy, **value substitution**, each time a cost is reduced, the customer gains a benefit too. This is what furniture manufacturer Ikea has done. The customer assembles the parts and does the shipping but has the furniture immediately – as well as the satisfaction of having built it. The company's showrooms are out of town – big units at lower rents. Yet for the customer this is a benefit too, because it means free parking and a playground for the kids. Shopping becomes a family outing as much as a furniture-buying errand.

In the third strategy, **value improvement** – removing the old furniture while installing the new – adds nothing to the cost of shipping while giving one benefit to the customer: getting rid of the old piece of stuff.

These three strategies are markedly different from one another. They are also notably different to the cost-cutting strategies most often used by companies: fewer benefits to the customers, fewer staff, less training of staff, fewer opening hours, less choice. This is illustrated in Figure 2.7.

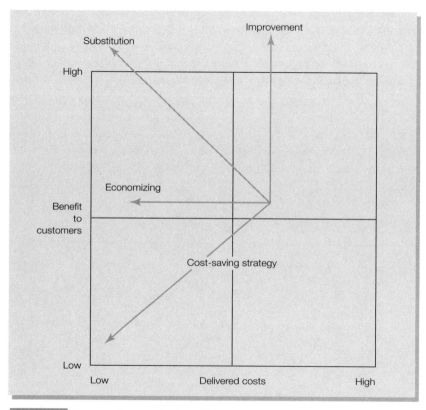

**Figure 2.7**    Decreased costs and benefit to customers

Most of the examples above illustrate value enhancement or expansion and extension. They are practiced by companies which have the intelligence to reduce their own costs while increasing benefits to their customer. A good example is Zurich's innovative total care approach to car insurance. Costs are reduced by economizing, while the benefits to customers are considerable. The company saves when experts no longer have to go to the repair shop where customers usually leave their cars; instead they drop in to preselected repair shops). While the cost of giving customers replacement cars is high, the company has negotiated a deal with Avis for these cars – and with repair shops for their services.

Benihana of Tokyo is an American restaurant chain which pioneered in-service teppanyaki. Customers sit on stools at tables designed for at least eight, and watch as a Japanese chef puts on a show of cutting, cooking and serving beef, chicken and shrimps. When finished, the chef will bow and the customer leaves. Compared with the classical restaurant, this experience represents both a saving in cost and added value (Figure 2.8).

|  | Buying ❯ | Preparation ❯ | Serving ❯ | Billing ❯ |
|---|---|---|---|---|
| **Cost savings for Benihana** | Three items only: beef, chicken, shrimps | Grilled, no kitchen; less rent | No waiter, tables of eight; less rent | One price; faster preparation and turnover; cheaper rent |
| **Added value for customer** | Perception of freshness | By the chef in front of customer. 'The theatre of the stomach' | 'Spoon feeding' by the chef; theatre | An exotic evening |

**Figure 2.8**  Benihana's outpacing strategy

# Value in business-to-consumer *vs* value in business-to-business

The concept of value and the value proposition can be detailed further, both to find meaningful differentiations for customers and to distinguish between business-to-consumer and business-to-business companies.

In **business-to-consumer**, the two sides of the equation can include one or some of the elements shown in Table 2.1.

**Table 2.1**   Possible value dimensions in business-to-consumer companies

|  | *Benefits* | *Costs* |
|---|---|---|
| Value improvement | ▪ Service performance characteristics<br>▪ Product performance characteristics<br>▪ Care<br>▪ Self-esteem (usually through the brand) | ▪ Price<br>▪ Return (with or without the package on the ticket)<br>▪ Ability to use it properly (e.g. washing machine)<br>▪ Find spare parts (e.g. battery for the cellphone)<br>▪ Getting rid of old one (e.g. when changing your carpet)<br>▪ Ease of repair (where do I have to go)<br>▪ Speed of reaction (car insurance) |
| Extension | ▪ Attention to specific needs (I am a vegetarian)<br>▪ Anticipating needs | ▪ Understanding the bill<br>▪ Getting responses to questions (call center)<br>▪ Wanting to change contract conditions (cellphone)<br>▪ Getting proper documentation<br>▪ Understanding documentation |
| Expansion | ▪ Ancillary services while you wait or as a reminder of your buy (e.g. coffee/tea while you wait for your one-hour glasses, and reminder after 2 years to have eye test)<br>▪ Surprises<br>▪ Wow experience | |

## In b-to-b businesses

With b-to-b, the story is a little bit different. This is because buyers are more 'rational' with the specifics that need to be addressed.

### Two examples

Tetra Pak sells packaging systems to the food and drink industry. Where are they on the scale of value described in Table 2.2? Probably at the third level, because they sell not only the package but also the machine that helps the customer to fill the package with liquid. They also include training on how to use the system. So Tetra Pak provides 'inputs' at an attractive cost of access and usage. The company's mission is 'A Tetra Pak should sell for more than it costs.'

**Table 2.2** Possible value levels in business-to-business services

|  | Benefits | Costs |
|---|---|---|
| Normal value | 1 Good product | At a 'good' price |
| Value improvement | 2 Better product or service quality performance | at a good cost:<br>– cost of usage<br>(use, training, disposal, etc.) |
| Value extension | 3 Better inputs (product, documentation, delivery schedule, other information) | – cost of access (ask questions/solve problems) |
| Value expansion | 4 Better customer product performance<br>5 Better customer business performance (helping customer improve their business through us) | – cost of change<br>– cost of transaction (administration, financing) |

On the other hand, some customers might ask the company to give market inputs and even consult on what new products would make a difference. Thanks to ease of handling, speed of filling and conservation quality of their packaging system, the customer can get a better price for their packaged goods. Here, the company states, 'We want our customers to see us as proactive business partners, using our global expertise in food processing and packaging to meet their needs, add value and deliver competitive advantage.'

Another example is Henkel, the German household and adhesive company. One of their industrial products was a coating for the automotive industry (level 1 or 2). However, to minimize pressure on price for the automobile manufacturers and to respond to their client's request for managing the surfacing of cars (almost like category management in retail), they got involved in moving from coating to body surface management. This includes improving the car's ability to resist scratches (a big irritation for consumers) and thus the company moves from level 1 to level 3/4.

The above description of value in b-to-b businesses has many implications including the kind of skills and competencies needed to deliver value, the selling skills necessary to convince the customer to buy, and the kind of pricing that the company is able to propose, as shown in Figure 2.9.

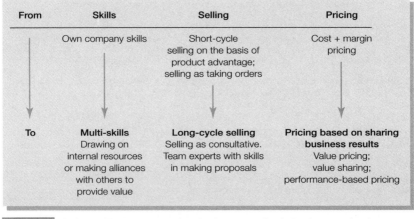

| From | Skills | Selling | Pricing |
|---|---|---|---|
| | Own company skills | Short-cycle selling on the basis of product advantage; selling as taking orders | Cost + margin pricing |
| To | **Multi-skills** Drawing on internal resources or making alliances with others to provide value | **Long-cycle selling** Selling as consultative. Team experts with skills in making proposals | **Pricing based on sharing business results** Value pricing; value sharing; performance-based pricing |

**Figure 2.9**   Skills required to move toward value expansion in business-to-business

## Does it pay to adapt the value proposition?

One of the key issues is how far we should go to adapt the value proposition to fit particular customer requirements. Variety can be the cause of more costs unless its supply is well thought out and designed.

- First of all, it pays to adapt if there are enough customers in each of the segments for which we think adaptation is required.

- Second, there are ways to separate the 'back office' service activities that are common (standardization), and thus fulfill the need for cost containment, and keep the front part of the service (differentiation).

- Finally, as in production of products, it is also possible to 'mass customize' a service, i.e. assemble modules of services together so that it becomes unique for the customer while benefiting from economies of scale for the service provider.

A few cases will illustrate the three possible directions: adapt per segment, separate back and front, mass customize.

## Adapt

**SKF** manufactures ball bearings. At some point, it discovered that, in fact, the after-sale market (i.e. the replacement of used bearings) was more lucrative than selling pure volume to original equipment manufacturers (OEMs). So it started to sell a bundle of services to factories that needed to change their bearings, be it sugar mills, oil refineries, equipment factories etc. The company sold the bundle of services either directly or via distributors. Thus, the company adapted to a different segment. They faced five essential choices to make it happen:

- Sell a package that would include a new set of bearings.
- Installation, training of the machine operator and lubrication of the machine to minimize the chances of unexpected breakdowns.
- Or it could sell two such 'trouble free operations' packages: one that would for instance secure 95 percent uptime, and the other 99 percent. The second operation would involve spare parts inventory on site, regular visits and warning systems directly linked to a call center, whereas the first operation would involve only fast repair.
- Or it could offer a menu of options 'à la carte', allowing each customer to choose together with the company what would best suit the needs of the customer.
- Or, finally, it could provide a unique solution to each customer depending on specific needs.

They chose the fourth alternative – more personalized than the first three but less costly than the last one. Thus each customer could self-select himself (with the help of the salesman!) to a reasonably close selection to his specific needs by picking from the *à la carte* list what suited him best.

## Separate the back office from the front

Alternatively, part of the service such as the back office can be standardized. For example, cellphone operators have the same network for all customers. However, heavy users or premium customers get a special hotline, special offers, an analytical bill, etc. This set of services provides more 'front office' value to the customer segment.

### Mass customize: modularization

Dell, the computer hardware company, states on its website that it builds to order: 'We provide customers with exactly what they want in their computer system through easy customer configuration and ordering. Build-to-order means that we don't maintain months of aging and expensive inventory. As a result, we typically provide our customers with the best pricing and latest technology for features they really want. Dell can offer this type of "tailor-made" product because it works with product modules that can be combined in a number of ways.'

'Dellizing' the service is the last possibility. For products with finite characteristics it is easy, but what about services? Most training and educational institutions and many knowledge-based companies are in fact 'Dellized.' Although the program proposed to a particular customer is unique, in fact it is only a unique combination of standard modules, well rehearsed and delimited, which have been put together to respond to the need of that particular customer.

## Does it pay to adapt?

Yes, as long as the adaptation cost is optimized by considerations of standardization through the options depicted in Figures 2.10, 2.11, and 2.12.

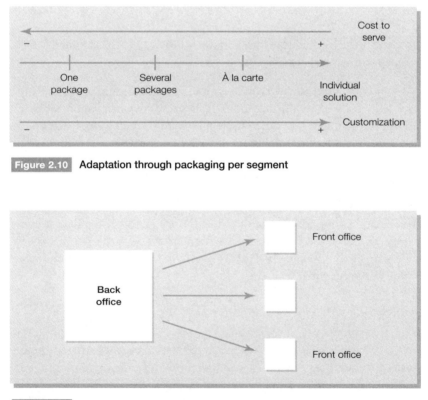

**Figure 2.10**  **Adaptation through packaging per segment**

**Figure 2.11**  **Adaptation by splitting front and back office**

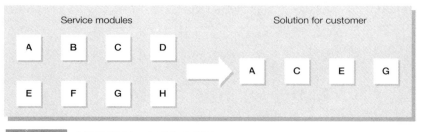

**Figure 2.12**  Adaptation by modularization

# Pricing adaptation in b-to-b companies: the building block approach

One of the toughest challenges in business-to-business companies is to adapt the value proposition according to the target customer and its need. It can get fairly complex when both products and services are required.

Take the example of HTS International GmbH, a leading system provider in Europe for washroom services and supplies and rental workwear. HTS International provides washroom products and service in 17 countries (soap and foam dispensers, air control systems and feminine hygiene disposal boxes, as well as the self-cleaning toilet seat 'Clean-Seat'). These can be put in one or several locations, such as in every store of a retail chain. Within each store, the machines can be placed in one of several places – for example in every bathroom on each floor. In addition, research done among their customers shows that no matter how many products and locations a client may have, some want price above all and, for that, are willing to be delivered consumables every two months without specifying which day of the week they are delivered, whereas others would like to be delivered at a certain hour, on a certain day, with automatic replacement of the dispenser, no down time, the possibility of changing dates and the amount of consumables from one time to the other (because of traffic), and certification that their hygiene is good.

The question is how to price those service requirements by on the one hand customizing as much as possible to be close to the customer, and on the other hand being able to standardize processes in such a way that it is manageable and deployable: for billing, for servicing, for responding to unanticipated needs, for changing conditions, etc.

This type of problem is common to many business-to-business firms. Essentially there are two ways to tackle it, with, as usual, a hybrid way in the middle.

The first option is to create three price levels and packages of services: Let's call them basic, standard and premium. Each could be offered to one of

three target customers, as depicted in Figure 2.13. Each package has a greater
number of services included.

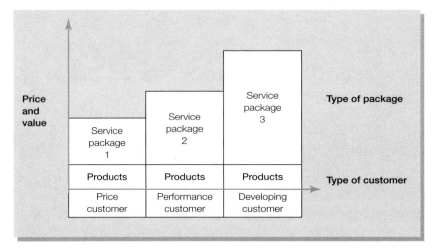

**Figure 2.13**    Price levels of packages of industrial services

| | | Hygiene certification |
|---|---|---|
| | | Automatic change of dispenser at customer request |
| | Annual check up | Additional emergency needs |
| | Delivery every 4 weeks | Delivery customized date/time |
| | Call center 9 to 5 | Emergency call center 24h/day |
| Basic products + delivery every 8 weeks | Standard | Premium |
| Products | Products | Products |
| Transactional customer | Strategic customer | Partner |

**Figure 2.14**    Added value pricing

The second alternative is to start from one end of the spectrum and add values (modules) to be chosen for each target customer, as depicted in Figure 2.14. And there could be even a hybrid version which is a mix of the previous ones wherein each of the three 'packages' is also modular – so that you can be even more flexible if required.

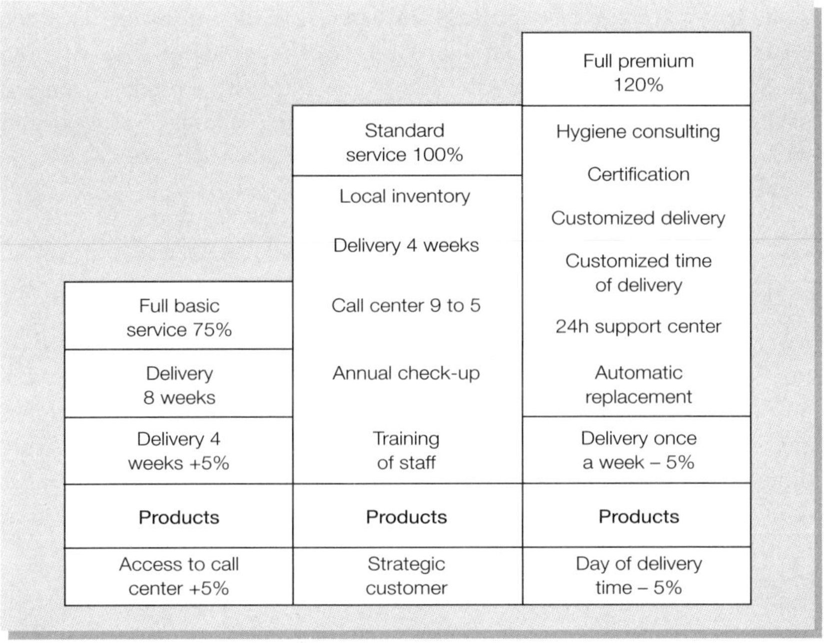

| Full basic service 75% | Standard service 100% | Full premium 120% |
|---|---|---|
| | | Hygiene consulting |
| | | Certification |
| | Local inventory | Customized delivery |
| | Delivery 4 weeks | Customized time of delivery |
| | Call center 9 to 5 | 24h support center |
| Delivery 8 weeks | Annual check-up | Automatic replacement |
| Delivery 4 weeks +5% | Training of staff | Delivery once a week – 5% |
| Products | Products | Products |
| Access to call center +5% | Strategic customer | Day of delivery time – 5% |

**Figure 2.15**    Flexible modularity pricing

In Figure 2.15, if a customer wants the basic package, they pay 75 percent of the standard service. However, if within the basic package they want to change to four weeks rather than use the eight weeks delivery cycle, they can add 5 percent, bringing it to 80 percent of the standard service. At the other end, the 'full treatment' would be 120 percent of the standard. By reducing their demands to weekly delivery rather than fully customized and specifying the day of delivery (such as every Wednesday) instead of the time (in the morning between 9 and 9:30 a.m.), they could reduce their bill to 110 percent.

On the one hand complexity in pricing can become the enemy of performance; on the other, customization can sometimes help grow the business. A modular approach to pricing can reconcile both.

# How to get your service concept known

Proposing a service to a customer and convincing them to buy is more difficult than selling a product. First, because a service is often intangible. Whether it is an insurance contract, a vacation trip to the Caribbean or a new SAP software system, you cannot touch, see, smell, sense or taste it before you buy it. Second, because even if you can get a good sense of what it will do for you (protect against disease, repair in case or failure, relax you on a vacation, or mess up your retail operations), you do not know whether the service provider will have the ability to serve! With a product, you can try it, test it, and buy a few before you commit to volume. You cannot test half a day of vacation, a quarter of an accident, or a tenth of SAP implementation in your company ... or a fifth of a haircut!

## Indirect communication works better to help the customer buy

As a result, any *indirect* method for communicating what the service can do for the customer is better than a direct method. By indirect, I mean any indirect way to tell your customers that your service offer is good, be it references, testimonials or articles written about you. The reason is that it is very difficult to tell yourself: Trust me I am the best repairman. Any indirect cues that will help the customer choose a particular service provider without test/trial are better than straight advertising.

Learning about the ability of the service provider to serve can come from different sources: references, testimonials, journalists, or past users. Any source is better than the provider itself. A fairly good reputation is indicated if past customers were so satisfied that they were willing to act as referees, testify, or talk to journalists or their friends and relatives about the company.

## Assessing a service provider pre-purchase also relies on peripheral cues or clues

As described in Chapter 1, I can assess a restaurant by the cleanliness of the windows, Federal Express by the speed with which they answer the phone, a maintenance contractor by the simplicity of their contract, the quality of a consultant by the intelligibility of their proposal, and a research lab by the quality of its publications. I can rate a retailer's merchandise by the care and knowledge of its salespeople; I can guess at the speed of decision of a bank by the tidiness of its offices. The service quality cues are not core to the service but can help a customer decide whether they want to buy or not. Those cues can be grouped into the following categories:

■ The five senses; these could also be described as the physical encounters (office, trucks, colors, layout of documentation, layout of proposals).

■ Peripheral service encounters: these are not at the core of the service provided but will help form an opinion of the type of service one can expect, such as:
  ■ ease of access;
  ■ welcome at reception;
  ■ speed of response to requests;
  ■ approachability of sales people;
  ■ speed to answer the phone.

■ Language:
  ■ ease of understanding;
  ■ use of terminology and jargon;
  ■ use of visuals to help.

These can either converge to give a potential customer a positive opinion of what will come next, as well as manage his expectations, or send such mixed signals that, at the end of his encounter with the cues, the customer is doubtful about the offer.

## The biggest challenge: convergence of signals sent to customers to avoid mixed signals

I was invited once by the CEO of a large Italian restaurant chain in Canada to give my views on customer service. Because of bad economic conditions, they had just launched a TV campaign saying 'we give you "encore and encore" (more and more), and, for the next few weeks, if you take a full meal we offer you a Caesar salad.' To test for a convergence of signals, I said 'But I did not order a Caesar salad.' There was no convincing reply except 'It is included in the menu.' Nobody had trained the waitress to feed in her presentation on the profusion and generosity positioning that was on TV (encore and encore) and say something like: 'Sir, our motto is encore and encore; we want to please you more than you expect. The Caesar salad is on the house! Encore and encore.' As a result, I am now not the best positive word-of-mouth ambassador for the company.

The problem is how to make sure that all functions and departments converge in identifying the signals that are sent to the customer, and whether they help persuade the customer to buy and return to become an ambassador for the service provider. In the above case, the head of marketing did his job with the media, with TV production, with creative people at the ad agency. Probably at the executive committee, he presented the campaign. Maybe a copy of it was sent to all restaurants. But the contact personnel who report to the head of operations did not participate in the effort, through lack of information and/or training. They could have done a lot more to transform dubious customers into ambassadors for the brand.

Table 2.3 summarizes some key elements of marketing cues.

**Table 2.3** Chase the cues you send to your customers to see if they converge – both to present your service and to demonstrate your ability to serve to your customers

*What do you want the customers to say about you (i.e. your service and your ability to serve)?*

|  | Converge | Diverge |
|---|---|---|
| The customer | | |
| meets your classical communication | | |
| – Advertising | ❏ | ❏ |
| – The press | ❏ | ❏ |
| – Leaflets | ❏ | ❏ |
| – Brochures – invitation of clients | ❏ | ❏ |
| The customer meets your documentation | | |
| – Proposals | ❏ | ❏ |
| – Contract layout | ❏ | ❏ |
| – Contract language | ❏ | ❏ |
| – Bills layout | ❏ | ❏ |
| – Bills label | ❏ | ❏ |
| – Internet layout | ❏ | ❏ |
| – Fax layout | ❏ | ❏ |
| The customer meets you 'physically' | | |
| – Vehicles | ❏ | ❏ |
| – Colors | ❏ | ❏ |
| – Court yard | ❏ | ❏ |
| – Lights | ❏ | ❏ |
| – Reception area | ❏ | ❏ |
| – Parking | ❏ | ❏ |
| – Building layout | ❏ | ❏ |
| – Offices layout | ❏ | ❏ |
| – Telephone speed | ❏ | ❏ |
| – Telephone message/music | ❏ | ❏ |
| Your company meets your staff | | |
| – 'Spiel'* of sales people | ❏ | ❏ |
| – 'Spiel' of after sales service people | ❏ | ❏ |
| – 'Spiel' of service delivery people | ❏ | ❏ |
| – 'Spiel' of intermediaries | ❏ | ❏ |
| – 'Spiel' at your call center | ❏ | ❏ |
| – Their clothes | ❏ | ❏ |

*By 'spiel' I mean type of arguments used and language expressed
*Source: Data from TARP (Quality Progress, March 2000)*

Finally, the topic should be presented in a fun and entertaining way, and be easy to grasp. For example, a daily routine sheet could be created for hotel hygiene staff, which specifies which rooms are to be serviced and when, includes cartoons. These cartoons represent levels of excellence in terms of room cleanliness and tidiness. This achieves two objectives at the same time:

■ They are easily understood (especially for people with reading difficulties).

■ They will look at it often and thus remember the principles outlined because it uses an existing tool (the routine sheet).

## Summary

To summarize, the process of bringing value to the customer starts by defining benefits that correspond to the particular need of a market segment. Identify the cost (including the price, effort, time) the customer will have to pay to profit from the service. The value proposition can be the same for all customers or adapted to different segments. The adaptation may take the form of different packages, *à la carte*, or complete customization. Pricing for such adaptation, especially for b-to-b companies, can take the form of a price per package, a basic price + a series of value added items or a modular approach, and, of course, complete individual pricing. The choice of adaptation *vs* standardization mode will have an impact on the cost of delivery of the service. However, the biggest impact on costs will come from a new look at the value-added chain, i.e. the series of activities that a company performs in order to always think of other ways to carry them, with fewer costs while increasing value for the customer.

Bear in mind: The more intangible the service is, the more it is necessary to communicate not only on the service itself but also on the potential ability to serve of the service provider. In this case, indirect methods perform better than direct ones.

## Don'ts

1 Don't start by thinking of value as the lifetime value the customer has for you. Only banks think that way. And they are neither customer – nor service-oriented! Think of value for the customer.

2 Don't reduce costs unless it maintains, keeps or even increases the benefits the customer gets. Otherwise you reduce value for the customers, and thus lose competitive advantage.

3 Don't underestimate the extra costs – besides selling price – both financial and non-financial, that the customer bears in using you! They can discount your value or the price the customer is willing to pay!

4 Don't put all your communication budgets into advertising! The more intangible your service, the less credible it is! Use more indirect communication.

5 Don't force all customers to buy the same value from you! Adapt it and still benefit from economies of scale.

6 Don't make your pricing over-complex! But let the customer see what difference it makes to choose one offer *vs* another one.

7 Don't sit on your laurels. Competition moves. Customer needs change. Periodically re-evaluate your value proposition to add, suppress, and change its dimensions.

# The 10 customer value questions

1 Who are your target customers? Do you have such targets?

2 What benefit(s) is each target customer is looking for?

3 Which beneficial strategic emphasis have you chosen: enhancement, extension, or expansion?

4 What 'costs' does your customer incur in using you? Are these costs too high? How can you reduce them?

5 Can you increase customer benefits and reduce your price and your costs at the same time? What outpacing strategy will you use: economizing, value substitution, or value improvement?

6 Where do you want to increase value in the relationship – selling, servicing, binding?

7 Should you adapt your value proposition to different segments: front office/customization/modules?

8 What communication means do you use to get your service concept known and how important is your indirect communication?

9 What do your peripheral cues say?

10 Are all your signals converging towards publicizing your value proposition?

# Delivering on customer value

**In 1999, Microsoft shifted** its emphasis from pushing new products to market to customer satisfaction. It realized that product innovation was not good enough to sustain its competitive advantage. Microsoft's first big effort in measuring customer satisfaction showed that there was a lot of room for improvement, and it quickly acted on hundreds of projects in every country to improve the delivery of its service. No matter how great your value proposition, delivering well on it is as important, if not more so, to get customers to come back and win new ones. How do you transform a great value proposition into an operational set of deliverables? How do you measure whether it fits both what the customer expects and what the organization is able to deliver? What impact does this have on customer satisfaction? These are the questions we will tackle in this chapter.

## The service concept

The service concept is the first step in transforming the value proposition into deliverables. Taking into account benefits for the customers and costs incurred (price, time, and effort) as well as our own cost of delivery, we can articulate the value in a service concept. This is usually summarized in few words: a one-line USP (unique selling proposition). The USP can also be the advertising slogan; examples include 'The theatre of the stomach' (the first advertising slogan used by Benihana of Tokyo), 'We are ladies and gentlemen serving ladies and gentlemen' (Ritz Carlton), 'We don't sell sandwiches, but solutions to your mood' (a sandwich shop in Arizona), and 'Eyeglasses in about an hour' (LensCrafters).

The USP can be developed into a 5–10 line commitment to customers, specifying the 'promise to the customer' – that is, the key benefits derived by the customer, taking into account the efforts and time necessary to get those benefits. Here are a few examples of such statements.

---

Medical diagnosis instruments

✔ We will only put into the market meticulously tested products.

✔ Our healthcare customer is both the professional and the end-user, and we will satisfy both needs.

✔ We will listen to their expertise, their reaction, and their satisfaction.

✔ To exceptional problems, we provide exceptionally fast solutions no matter what the cost is.

✔ Customers will get credit when they help us find new solutions.

---

An office-furniture maker sees it from the customer's point of view

✔ Respect the logic of my decision.

✔ Respect my time constraints.

✔ Make it easy for me to buy.

✔ Respect me as a person.

✔ Help me create an ambience.

✔ Be my partner in presenting my investment.

✔ Respect my budget.

✔ Recognize your mistakes and take care of them at no charge.

---

A one hour photo processing shop

✔ To say 'good morning/afternoon' and smile.

✔ To meet the deadline given to the client.

✔ To process all photographs as if they were our own.

✔ To immediately re-print unsatisfactory photographs.

✔ To never say 'No.'

✔ To offer a wide range of service.

✔ To be available for and attentive to the customer as soon as the store opens.

✔ To always have a clean and welcoming store for receiving customers.

✔ To be impeccably dressed for our clients.

✔ To listen and advise.

✔ To be the first to open and the last to close in the mall.

---

A restaurant chain

✔ To be able to have a good meal, centered around red meat: grilled, always tender, always fresh, always tasty, and chosen from a wide range of good-quality cuts at the right price.

✔ To always be served generously and to enjoy, at your own speed, a meal – meat and accompanying vegetables of your choice – the preparation and presentation of which are flawless.

✔ To always be welcomed warmly, known and recognized, put at ease, guided, and then accompanied to your table with a pleasant manner and good humor.

✔ To relax in an atmosphere that is always cheerful, in a clean, tidy restaurant with an attractive décor.

---

Finally this promise can be reinforced by the type of super service guarantee discussed in Chapter 4. Such guarantees involve the attitude of the server and self-imposed penalties on the provider when the service is sub-standard.

By the way, this philosophy also applies to support and administration departments which must commit to providing an excellent service to the other sections of the company. Illustrated below is how the human resources department of a retail chain expressed that commitment.

---

A human resources department

✔ To be available, to welcome them in a kindly manner with good humor.

✔ To assist them in legal and social matters, in questions of insurance, and administrative formalities.

> ✔ To give support for hiring and training and to get quality personnel.
>
> ✔ To inform about the life of the group and existing inhouse talents.
>
> ✔ To give precise and rapid answers (within 24 hours).

Those commitments should be published. Internally, publication can take the form of posters on the door of each department – even each office. I have seen some go to the lengths of expressing such commitment in verse or calligraphically. Such publication has two advantages:

1 Customers, whether internal or external, can readily see what is being offered (or not) and are in a position to remonstrate with the staff if the reality does not live up to the promise.

2 They are a pleasant way to remind staff of what they stand for.

Let me give you an example, written in verse, for the group managing director of an international retail group (my translation):

*My first trait, it's clear:*
*To question your ideas,*
*To see what happened in the past*
*So that I may help you advance.*

*My second – who'd have guessed?*
*Is to prepare best*
*Signs safe and sure*
*And develop their allure.*

*My third, then, is to define*
*Strategic options which in time*
*Will construct the future*
*Foundations of our great adventure*

*Overall, you can see,*
*It's scored musically:*
*Ambitions, talents, soul*
*All striving for one goal.*

A British water supplier has prepared a statement that covers the following areas: appointments, complaints, paying for water by meter, paying your bill, disconnecting the water supply, the quality of water supply, sewerage services, rationing in a drought, water pressure.

Otis has prepared a promise covering reliability, responsiveness, communication, care, and assurance.

## Specifying a detailed level of excellence

The level of service the organization is willing to give has to be spelled out in greater detail. It needs to be developed into service standards that will make your company's promise tangible and concrete, and cover all aspects of the relationship with the customer.

For example, one of the commitments made by Otis is reliability – the capacity to maintain performance and maximize availability. This prompts other questions: What does the commitment mean for downtime, for speed, and for stopping within a specified number of inches from the floor?

For the water supply company, continuous supply is a commitment. If temporary cuts occur due to repair work or other causes, what duration is tolerable? This is why a promise of quality must be translated into service standards which set the norms or the level of excellence. For Otis, the promise may be quantified as a one-hour response time. For the water supply company it might be: 'If we need to turn off the water supply to your property for one to four hours, we will let you know at least 12 hours beforehand.'

Those standards should cover all interfaces between the customer and the company at each phase of the relationship, as well as all types of encounter between the customer and the company. Standards are best expressed by starting each sentence with the phrase 'The client / the customer will…' (get his drink in less than 5 minutes and his bill with his coffee).

To help a company define those standards, I have found it useful to identify the steps the customer goes through when using a service, and divide the encounters into three categories:

- Physical encounters.
- Transactional encounters.
- Interaction encounters.

These encounters cover all areas where levels of excellence should be identified. This is depicted schematically in Figure 3.1, where the norms of excellence can be specified for each cell.

| Steps the customer goes through (example) | Selects us | Buys from us | Gets delivered | Uses us |
|---|---|---|---|---|
| Physical encounters | ? | ? | ? | ? |
| Transactional encounters | ? | ? | ? | ? |
| Interaction encounters | ? | ? | ? | ? |

**Figure 3.1**  Identifying levels of excellence in customers' encounters with the company.

The term 'physical encounter' encompasses all experiences the customer has of a company's physical settings: buildings, documentation, signage, and merchandise. Standards of excellence in the domains of cleanliness, atmosphere, clarity, transparency, ambience belong to the first group.

A 'transactional encounter' involves all the interfaces the customer has with respect to your systems. In this arena one defines levels of excellence in terms of delivery, speed, absence of hassle, information given to users, and performance of service.

'Interactional encounters' involve interfaces with employees: levels of excellence with respect to responsiveness, proactiveness, care, and communication. Solving problems on the spot also belongs in this category.

And in fact service becomes excellent when all three types of encounter are congruent and well balanced.

Suppose you are a local trader, and go to a bank to be welcomed in a plush private room with leather armchairs. No matter how good the proposed loan rate, you will probably perceive it as too high; you will be convinced that the money goes on expensive furniture rather than on good deals.

Say you read the beautiful and simple advertising for a new machine that will help you lose weight (physical encounter). Then you look at the manual – it is complicated (another physical encounter). So you ask the sales representative some questions, and do not get a satisfactory answer (interaction encounter). When you try to order by phone, the line is always busy (transactional). What is the net impression?

# How many service standards, how detailed, and for whom?

How many standards you formulate depends on the complexity of the service offered and the level of the organization at which they are developed. In an airport, the statement 'Fifteen minutes to get your baggage in proper condition' may mean different things at different levels of the organization. For the airport manager it signifies five minutes to offload and take care of baggage, another five minutes to carry it (not losing it on the tarmac), and then five minutes to put it (carefully) on the right conveyor belt. Here one level of excellence really implies three.

At corporate level, a maximum of 50 standards of excellence should be drawn up. These could be translated down the line into 1,000 to 2,000 statements for complex service concepts such as a theme park, which includes hotels, catering, entertainment, and rides.

Detailing a standard means not simply defining the level of excellence required (the customer will get a hamburger in two minutes, or a loan in 24 hours), but what to do and how to get it done. The more experienced, stable and educated your staff, the less meaningful it is to specify what to do and how to do it; just say why (expressed customer benefit), and leave the initiative to the teams. However, in other cases you will need at least a base of the 'what' and 'how' questions in order to get new employees started. Let us consider the role of the 'animateur' at Club Med. You could limit standards to the following:

■ The customer will be entertained during the daytime.

■ Or be more specific (why).

■ The customer will find diverting, amusing events at breakfast, before and after lunch, and in the evening ('why' in more detailed form).

To those statements you could add the following:

■ A 'bag of tricks': that is, the 50 small events that have worked best in the past that you can safely use during the daytime (what).

Or you could add:

■ The tricks are best used with the help of the team. We have specified for each what props are needed as well as who should be with you, how many other staff members are needed, and how to recognize a customer on whom tricks should not be played (how).

If we stay at the first level, we assume the animateur will know what to do and when. All we want is continuous entertainment, not just at night. The means belong to the entertainer, who will learn on the job or from previous experience. As we move down the items, we start to be more specific about when the diversions should take place, what form they will take, and how they are to be arranged. We get to the point where we can train an unskilled or inexperienced entertainer by providing a safety net. Later on, the animateur will become more skilled, and do better or new things. Therein lies the dilemma of any service organization. How much empowerment – or initiative in deciding what to do and how – should be given? How much investment must be made up-front to equip the team to perform a minimum service? This dilemma is, of course, linked to people management – the seventh secret – as we shall see later.

No matter how detailed you want to be or need to be, what's certain is that standards of excellence:

- should be explicit;
- should be created by your best people;
- should be shared with all the teams (services, administration as well as field);
- should be used in all induction seminars;
- should be called to mind as often as possible through internal communication campaigns (let's beat the standard);
- Should be updated and reviewed every year or two to eliminate, consolidate, add and refresh.

## Service quality measurement

'If you can't measure it, then you can't manage it,' according to the old management maxim. But first it is essential to define precisely what is to be measured, and the reasons for measuring it. What is the company's aim?

- To improve what it is doing at present (today's quality of service).
- To evaluate customers' ideal preferences in order to plan for the future.

Is the company comparing its present performance with what it did in the past, or is it seeking to outdo competitors by comparing its service with what they do? Or is it measuring itself against world class companies? Is the organization looking at progress in terms of how the customer perceives the quality it delivers (perceived quality), or is it attempting to measure progress in terms of what is really delivered (actual quality)? Are you talking of progress for all customers, potential customers, some customers, or reducing the risk of losing customers?

Depending on the company's objectives, the measurements will differ in content, perspective (what they are compared with or measured against), and target.

In summary, be clear about what you are looking for (see Figure 3.2).

| Domain / Point of view | Value proposed to the customer | Value delivered to the customer |
|---|---|---|
| Quality in fact | New performance levels to make a difference to customers | Performance indicators for the existing service as delivered |
| Perceived quality | • New dimensions of value desired by customers<br>• Benefits sought by customers<br>• Image of what is being offered (especially for non-customers) | • Current customer dissatisfaction/satisfaction with dimensions of quality that are perceived to be important<br>• Customer complaints/compliments<br>• Improvement opportunities perceived by customers |

**Figure 3.2**  Decide what to measure

# Measurement tools

For each objective there is a tool: here are some of the techniques for measuring different aspects of customer service.

■ Trade-off (or conjoint) analysis allows customers to identify which combination of features in a product/service they prefer, and prioritize accordingly (for instance, by choosing speed of delivery rather than additional options when buying a car, or deciding between width of seat versus amenities when choosing an airline). In 1996, British Airways embarked on major research into the future needs of its customers. Thirty focus groups and a quantitative conjoint analysis carried out with the help of 2,500 customers gave the airline some idea of what it should be doing in the future.

■ Qualitative interviews with existing or potential customers, or an analysis of customer complaints (what, where, when) may highlight what the customers are looking for and what may be missing in the product/service currently offered.

These qualitative interviews are also often used to prepare a sound customer satisfaction survey – that is, a questionnaire in which one makes sure that all dimensions of service are included and expressed in the customer's language. Such questionnaires also serve as a basis for quantitative trade-off analysis.

Qualitative surveys are very powerful. They are listening posts, giving valuable intelligence about the attitudes of a company's customers. For large organizations, they can also be used to provide effective customer segmentation. By analyzing the information provided, a company may be able to classify customers, grouping them in segments according to their wishes and priorities. Segmentation can be used to improve service, on the basis of the customers' expressed wishes. To take another example, research with focus groups at Disney found that there were four distinct types of customer, defined according to their expectations. These are depicted graphically in Figure 3.3.

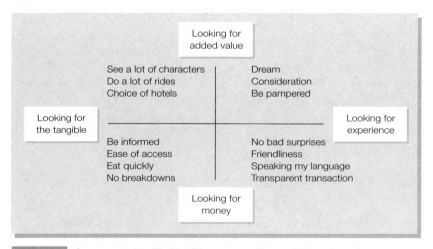

**Figure 3.3** Customers classified by Disney according to their expectations

If you have limited resources or time, go for the qualitative measurements, as they are the richest!

Indicators such as delays in delivery, failure rates, and breakdowns can tell you what is going wrong without having to ask customers. On the other hand 'ghost shopper' checklists such as International Research Mystery Shopper surveys, in which researchers act as customers to test the response of an organization's staff and systems, measure how the company is doing against its own current standards.

Finally, customer satisfaction surveys, whether face-to-face, by post or telephone, permit an assessment of how customers perceive the company with respect to the products or services it currently provides.

In summary, Figure 3.4 plots the main techniques described in this section.

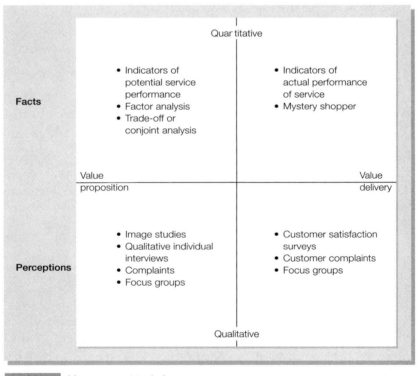

**Figure 3.4**   **Measurement techniques**

# Which customers are we talking about?

There are three main steps that a customer goes through when using a service: the purchase, use of product or service, then a repurchase. The process is depicted graphically in Figure 3.5.

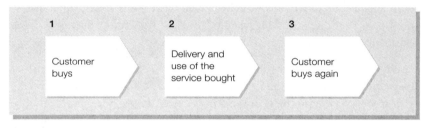

**1**

Customer
buys

**2**

Delivery and
use of the
service bought

**3**

Customer
buys again

**Figure 3.5**   Steps that a customer goes through

Logically, we should then measure customer quality of service at each step.

- Are the customers satisfied with the company's efforts to help them buy?
- Are the customers happy about the delivery and/or the use of the service?
- Did the customer's satisfaction lead to their continuing to use us, and to repeat purchases?

Unfortunately, the customers at various stages of the process may not necessarily be the same people. There are those who buy and those who do not. At renewal time, one finds those who have bought again, and those who have not (the 'lost customers'). So, logically, a good measurement should include all three groups:

**1**   prospective customers who did not buy;

**2**   customers who did buy; and

**3**   lost customers.

From the first category – prospective customers – the company may learn what goes wrong with the attracting/selling process – why some potential customers have perceived it as inadequate, and did not purchase. What would make people buy? This input will help improve the 'sales process.' It does not rely solely on feedback from those who have bought to assess either the perceived quality of current sales activities, or what new sales activities should be put in place to convert non-buyers. When considering potential customers in this context, one should also distinguish between those who come to your company and decide not to buy, and those who have never approached the company, but who are part of your target market (see Figure 3.6).

| Did not approach us | Approached us and did not buy |
|---|---|
| Evaluate our communication and value proposition | Evaluate the selling process |

Figure 3.6    Potential customers

In the first instance, image studies (which indicate what image we have compared with other suppliers and on which attribute we are weaker) and preference studies (what benefits our potential customers preferred from other suppliers) will do the best job. In the second case one can use customer satisfaction surveys, focusing on the selling process. Questions could include whether the sales representative was welcoming, professional and listening; and whether the proposal was adequate, timely, clear, and so on.

Alternatively a company could use ghost shoppers making pseudo-buys. Researchers are given a constant scenario and trained to act as customers attempting to buy from your company. Then you record what happens. This technique provides valuable information; it can also be used to compare your selling process with that of the competition.

It is amazing how few companies talk to the majority of the people who could evaluate their 'selling process.' In industry, generally you win one out of four bids. Yet companies will ask only the customers who bought to evaluate their sales representatives, documentation and the like. The customer who has bought should feel pretty satisfied. But there are three others who have been prepared to spend time with your organization, and remain uninterviewed! As far as possible, I use real customers to carry out ghost buys: consumers for consumer services and friends at companies for industrial products. The idea is to get their gut reactions and impressions – not just the consultant's critical eye.

Then, of course – and this is what most companies do – evaluate how current customers perceive the service they get. This will provide useful leads on how to improve delivery, after sales service, follow-up, and so on. A company selling complex systems to large businesses will need to break down its measurements – one for users, one for decision makers, one for buyers – as they are all involved in using the service.

Finally, finding out from lost customers the reasons for their dissatisfaction or defection is a very good indicator of potential future customer losses, as illustrated in Figure 3.7. These two columns compare the satisfaction ratings of existing customers with various service parameters with those of lost customers. Assuming all parameters are of equal weight, one can immediately identify the 'follow-up' category as a key determinant in losing a customer. Thus, any movement to the left of the 'follow-up' dimension on the left-hand column (existing customers) would give the company an important danger signal.

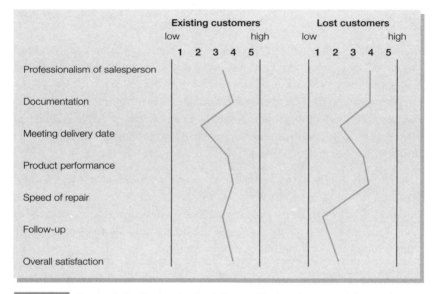

**Figure 3.7** How satisfaction levels of existing and lost customers might compare

I have done more than 150 customer satisfaction measurements for large companies in Europe; those which have measured the satisfaction of the 'non-customers' are rare. In other words, most companies fail to use potential visitors, non-visitors, non-buyers or lost customers to improve their sales efforts. They do not get data on lost customers to prevent them from losing more. Therefore one should ensure that not only existing customers, but also those who did not buy and those who were lost, are investigated.

# Focus on the mystery shopper: facts and perceptions

Mystery shoppers (or ghost shoppers) can be used to improve quality, both perceived and real. Many companies use the technique to check whether standards of quality of service are indeed met. For instance, the McDonald's QSC (Quality, Service, Cleanliness) standards are frequently measured by ghost shoppers. Checklists are used. The mystery shopper will tick boxes: yes or no, observed, non-observed, works, does not work, and so on. There is little interpretation or room for personal inputs where overall impressions, feelings and so on are concerned. This technique is best used when the service provided is not too complex, when in one visit the whole service can be witnessed and controlled, and when standards of service are very well defined. It can help assess:

■ How much variance there is now between the designed quality of service and that delivered.

■ What areas to focus on in training.

A certain minimum number of visits is required to give some reasonable significance to the measurements, and take into account exceptional events (lack of staff due to sickness, for example). Five visits per site per measurement will be more credible than one. This is often used in retailing, restaurant chains, hotel chains, and transportation. Mystery shopping requires as many metrics as possible, and a standard approach to avoid disagreement and anger on the part of the team measured. For instance, the question of cleanliness might be phrased in a questionnaire as: 'Clean – Yes/No.' This can be answered by observing specifics such as the number of papers or cigarettes on the floor in the reception area rather than by subjective judgment.

However, mystery shoppers can also be used in another way to get closer to perceived service quality. Here one starts with a carefully designed scenario and a role that the shopper will play. The script will specify who the shopper is, what he or she wants and needs, the shopper's behavior, what interactions are to be tested, and how far the shopper will go to test staff. As well as creating the role play, there is a need to make sure that as much as possible of the visit (or phone call) is recorded so that all the details can be captured. These might include:

■ sequence of events;

■ overall impression;

■ delight, likes, dislikes, hates;

■ impact on behavior; and

■ impact on feelings.

Instead of being translated quantitatively as a series of positive and negative answers, this way of doing things results in a very qualitative report. It is a 'mini case study' that will be used in debriefing with the controlled team, and in training or coaching.

Disneyland Paris uses both types of mystery shopper. Executives, many of them from administration, finance or other support areas, do the straightforward quantitative surveys. They visit the park and the hotels and rate the service on five dimensions:

- cleanliness;
- working conditions;
- working time;
- information given;
- proactiveness (presence or otherwise).

The executives answer 'yes' or 'no' and include some comments. For the operating teams, it is a measure of the standard achiever. For the executives it provides an opportunity to assess and witness quality first hand.

Volunteer cast members do the second type of survey – qualitative research. They have a scenario and test it in a particular ride or restaurant. This helps the local team improve qualitatively; it is also used as training material in Disney University. Finally the volunteers are sensitized even further on what it is to be a customer – whoops, sorry! – a guest.

# Customer satisfaction surveys: level and frequency

If satisfaction is measured at corporate level only, then any satisfaction or dissatisfaction at local level (site, business unit, region, or function) will probably not be acted upon. For instance, suppose the overall satisfaction rating of customers is based on two dimensions:

1 Product offering.

2 Speed of delivery from each of five warehouses.

Whereas the first may be a corporate issue, the second issue could depend on the procedures and behavior of staff at a number of different warehouses. Thus, to be action-oriented, a customer satisfaction measurement should be performed at the level where action can be taken. Furthermore, the company needs to present the data in such a manner that local management can act on the dimensions of service that contribute most to overall satisfaction, as shown in Figure 3.8.

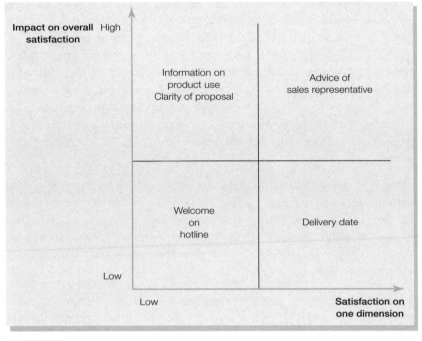

**Figure 3.8** Priorities for satisfaction improvement

If you examine Figure 3.8 you will come to an important conclusion. You will see that improving the quality of information that is given to customers on product use should be a company's first priority. For sheer impact on customer satisfaction, this is matched only by clarity of proposal. Since the purpose of measurement is to achieve action, I have already stressed that measurements should be taken at a level in the organization where something can be done. Related to this is another issue: how often such measurements should be taken. This in turn is linked to sample size and the cost of information.

The 'right' frequency is the one that allows significant improvements to be made between two measurements, and one that keeps up the pressure so that customer satisfaction remains a top priority. This will, of course, depend on the industry (for improvement cycle time) and company culture.

Xerox has a battery of measurements serving different needs; the frequency with which they are carried out varies from test to test. Every customer is asked to rate Xerox as well as its competitors. This competitive benchmarking also helps identify where Xerox is doing less well than its competitors, and enables the company to act upon any flaw identified.

After a new product or service is launched, a survey is taken to identify any problems customers might face. This serves as an early warning system. Other companies like Renault use heavy users such as taxi drivers for feedback on new products, since they will encounter problems before others. At Xerox, a 'post-installation' survey is done 7–50 days after the installation of a machine to allow the customer to respond quickly. Another survey is conducted 50 days later. Monthly surveys are carried out in the US involving 40,000 randomly selected customers. The target levels are 50 percent users, 25 percent decision makers, and 25 percent administration workers.

In today's world of one-to-one relationships – or at the very least, segmented customer groups – customer satisfaction must be covered not only by site or business unit and area of responsibility but also per segment. Microsoft's worldwide initial customer satisfaction survey involved 250,000 customers. Results were presented by country and within each country by customer segment.

# Genuinely wanting feedback from customers or pretending to?

Air France has been measuring customer satisfaction on its flights for quite some time. However, from their method you might be suspicious of the results.

First of all, although the crew has been given a list of seats whose occupants are to be approached, it can sometimes seem that the steward or stewardess goes to another seat because he or she does not like the look of the passenger in the assigned seat. Then, if you ask for a pen to fill the questionnaire in, you receive the reply 'Sorry, I only have one.'

The survey is introduced along the following lines: 'Management has asked us to ask you to fill in this customer satisfaction questionnaire.' Which hardly demonstrates the staff's full commitment to the endeavor – you don't get the impression that they're eagerly awaiting your feedback, to say the least!

You are then given four questionnaires in four colors, in four languages. This does not demonstrate cost-consciousness, nor environmental awareness. Much better would have been simply to ask, 'Which language do you speak?' Or they could even use some initiative and note which newspaper you are reading.

Your 'experience' (or should I say ordeal) is not finished, since 60 percent of the questions are designed to give information to Air France's marketing people. 'Where did you board the plane? Where are you landing?' They should know this already! 'How many times do you fly per year?' This is not asking for feedback; this is statistical data. Finally, if you don't take the initiative to give the survey back, no one asks for your 'valued' inputs, because the plane is coming in to land and there's no time for the crew to collect it!

So, what are the key elements for seeking and receiving genuine feedback on customer satisfaction?

■ Demonstrate your eagerness to want the customer's feedback.

■ Avoid the word 'questionnaire' – present it as a genuine interest to improve. Personalize it (language used, name of the customer written on it). This can raise the response rate from 5 or 10 percent to 90 percent if the rest of the list is followed.

■ Make it easy to answer: Provide a table, a chair and a pen.

■ Leave plenty of room for qualitative comments (suggestions, priorities seen from customer viewpoint etc.) and cut down on quantitative ticking of boxes

■ Do not mix feedback with collecting marketing data.

■ Use a scale that minimizes cultural bias and is clear to customers. If you are a world-class company, use the following: completely satisfied, very satisfied, satisfied, mildly satisfied, unsatisfied – otherwise very satisfied, satisfied, mildly satisfied, dissatisfied, very dissatisfied. Use the top of the box to express satisfaction, e.g. 90 percent to 100 percent rather than quantitative scores such as 4.2 or 8.7.

■ Collect feedback from everyone who can judge the quality of your service – i.e. users, prescribers, decision makers, purchasers. In this case, to get an overall picture for a particular customer, obtain an overall satisfaction rating, answers to a core common series of questions, and then, answers to specific questions for specific parts of your client or customer organization.

■ Take the time to collect.

■ Give feedback to customers on the results of the surveys.

■ Do not 'over'-survey; spend more time and resources fixing the problems, and resurvey once you have improved.

# Beyond customer satisfaction surveys: taking into account the voice of the customer at all times

Satisfaction surveys are great tools for measuring where one stands quantitatively. However there are some pitfalls:

- **The numbers game** = getting to a number is vital, e.g. 4.2 or 8.7. If we achieve this we feel safe! The voice of the customer only serves to get to a number that will be put into the annual scoreboard. As time goes by, nobody remembers what this number means, or what explains it!

- **The quantitative scale issue**. Say we get a score of 4.2 (or 8.1). What does that mean? I prefer to use the percentage of completely satisfied, very satisfied, satisfied, mildly satisfied, and dissatisfied (only one negative as it is enough!). This says more to everybody about how much we need to improve. A rating of 8 (on a scale of 1 to 10) or 4 (on a scale of 1 to 5) helps in putting statistical tables together, but is meaningless when assessing the effort necessary to improve.

## The multiple contact issue

For complex businesses, there is no one contact for each client but several within the client organization. Whose point of view are we interested in – buyers, users, or decision makers? To solve this problem, one can either have several surveys (one for each contact), or a survey which includes a common section for all and a separate part for each type of contact.

## The low response rate issue

'People are fed up with filling in questionnaires' I am told when I promote customer satisfaction measurement. Not so. I have always managed to get a response rate of between 80 and 95 percent in 'business-to-business' companies and between 40 and 90 percent in 'business-to-consumers'. So how do you do this?

- First, by presenting the exercise not as a routine questionnaire, given only because management wants it, but by *genuinely* making sure that it is presented as a means to improve things.

- Second, by not using the questionnaire as a means to *collect data* on customers (asking for their e-mail address for instance). It signals that the company is more interested in its database than in receiving input about how to improve importance.

■ Third, by demonstrating that *commitment* to listen to customers by leaving blank space for them to give suggestions and comments, rather than just asking them to tick boxes.

■ Fourth, by choosing the most *convenient* way for the customer to give their feedback: whether that be by Internet, telephone, face-to-face for business, assisted face-to-face, or by phone (and do not forget to have a pen ready).

## Measuring is of no use

There is no reason to measure for measurement's sake. It is true that a good end-of-project review or a genuine, face-to-face assessment can achieve more than a quantitative questionnaire. However, on a periodical basis, a broader viewpoint can give additional feedback. In fact, companies which have few clients are usually involved in complex long-term transactions and relationships. With 50 clients, there could be between 5 and 20 contacts within each firm (plus the users) – or 1000 contacts. And thus many sources of feedback. The frequency of measurement must be such that, between two measurements, there is enough time to act and improve. That way the next measurement can assess both the performance of what has been improved and what remains to be done. Thus a phone survey of all client contacts could be carried out every two years. Tetra Pak started to do this in 2000 for each of their clients in each country. Figure 3.9 shows how the company displays clients after measuring the customer satisfaction of contacts within each organization.

## Other sources of customer voices

Customer feedback is not limited to satisfaction measurement. Other ways to obtain feedback include the following:

■ Spend a day with the customer.

■ Listen to complaints (and compliments).

■ Invite customers into your factory and your office.

■ Involve customers in your quality improvement teams, project teams, and R&D tests.

- Involve lead users in quality improvement (e.g. car manufacturers asking cab drivers to give feedback) .

- Develop a users' club that meets on a regular basis.

- Spend time with front line people: call centers, field force, etc.

- Have multiple sources of feedback for a customer. For instance, if you are a hotel doing seminars, obtain feedback from participants and from the organizer, and from the trainers and consultants who conduct those seminars.

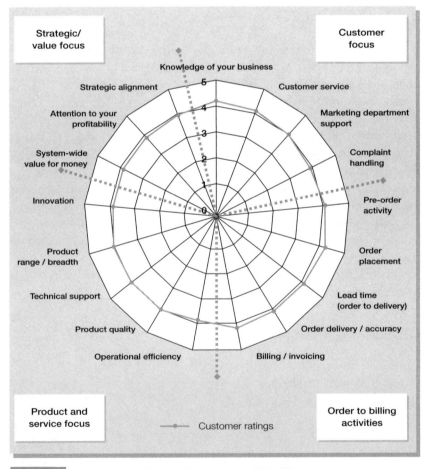

**Figure 3.9**   Tetra Pak visualization of customer satisfaction

*Source: K. Kashani, IMD, Tetra Pak (B) case*

# An overall index: mixing perceptions and facts

Some companies have developed sophisticated methods to realize a vision: a single, unified index that will finally capture whether a company is doing the job correctly in both real and perceived terms. At Motorola it is 'six-sigma', sigma being a measurement of variance (1 standard deviation from the mean). Six-sigma corresponds to 1 error out of 10 million possible. So for all departments, a list of defects is made and the actual defects are measured. Those effects can relate to product but also to service. At Renault, the system is called the 162 mark; it applies to product. Each defect at kilometer zero has a point system, and each defect is weighed. When the factory reaches a score of 162, there have been no defects.

A remarkable use of quality indicators is provided by the Office of Water Services in England and Wales (OFWAT). Every year since 1992 this body has monitored the service provided by all 17 local water companies and 10 water and sewerage companies. The overall indicator runs at a score of 250 points for the best and 150 for the worst. It includes indicators on water pressure, interruptions to supply, hosepipe bans, water quality, flooding incidents, written complaints, billing errors, meter reading, telephone access and speed of response, repairs, debtor and disconnection policies, compensation, leakage, sludge disposal, sewage treatment, and so on. For each area there is an objective criterion of quality. Such criteria include the percentage of written complaints answered within 10 days, with 98 percent being considered good, 95–98 percent acceptable, and less than 95 percent as needing improvement. Another measure is properties per 100,000 at risk of being flooded by sewage more than twice every 10 years.

At FedEx quality indicators per dimension of service include late arrivals of mail, mistakes in sorting, and time taken to answer a query. Results for each category are added to make a total. The number of complaints in each category is also counted, and these subtotals are combined with the total to make an index. This system may be intellectually appealing – perhaps the engineer's dream – but it fails to capture what remains a key feature of measurement: how to take suitable action to improve service. To act you do not want aggregate data: You want details. If it is perfectly legitimate at corporate level to want one single index showing progress, you need deseg-regated data to make that progress!

# Does it pay to improve customer satisfaction?

Perhaps this question should have been the first one asked! It is amazing how few companies know, or estimate, how much one extra point of customer satisfaction will bring in either as extra sales or as profit.

For most companies, not knowing means not working on customer satisfaction improvements; for others it means under-investing. For a few, it means over-investing in satisfaction improvement. In fact, it is both conceptually and practically feasible to estimate the linkage between customer satisfaction and company profit, and it is quite useful to help define priorities. Let us take the following example of a retailer, for whom we got the results shown in Figure 3.10.

|  | Completely satisfied | Very satisfied | Satisfied | Fairly satisfied | Dissatisfied |
|---|---|---|---|---|---|
| Ratings | 20% | 30% | 35% | 10% | 5% |
| Average purchase | 100 euro | 95 euro | 50 euro | 30 euro | 25 euro |

**Figure 3.10**  Customer satisfaction levels

Is it better to convert those who are 'very satisfied' to being 'completely satisfied', or would it be preferable to make the 'fairly satisfied' 'satisfied'? Which will pay off more? On what levels must we act to move our customers from one column to the other? Are they the same? What investment should we make?

To answer these questions, you need a linkage between levels of satisfaction, underlying causes of satisfaction/dissatisfaction classified by level, and some form of link between level of satisfaction and buying behavior, or customer profit contribution over time (customer life-time value). This linkage can and must be found by looking at the past behavior of customers. Ask whether those who were more satisfied stayed longer with the company and bought more than the others did. Are the better satisfied more likely to buy from the company in the future? These estimates are necessary to find the proper leverage points. Figure 3.11 summarizes 130 surveys carried out in Europe for selected industries.

In effect, and depending on the industry, sales increases between 3 and 33 percent are possible. As seen from Figure 3.11, the scores vary widely.

| | Satisfaction | | Recommendation | | Repurchase | | Between worst and best Potential for progress | |
|---|---|---|---|---|---|---|---|---|
| | Best score | Worst score | Best score | Worst score | Best score | Worst score | Recommendation | Repurchase |
| Automobile | 98% | 71% | 86% | 23% | 44% | 11% | 330% | 400% |
| Banking | 96% | 67% | 50% | 29% | n/a | n/a | 90% | |
| Business-to-business services | 94% | 67% | 90% | 44% | 87% | 38% | 200% | 120% |
| Hospitality | 87% | 78% | 78% | 20% | 90% | 15% | 400% | 400% |
| Insurance | 90% | 52% | 70% | 21% | 66% | 26% | 320% | 350% |
| Retail | 95% | 61% | 83% | 49% | 76% | 51% | 90% | 20% |

**Figure 3.11**    **Satisfaction and purchasing behavior**

Companies often ask who they should compare themselves with, and what constitutes a good score. Having worked both for world class companies and 'normal retail' firms, I have found that it is useful for world class companies to adjust upwards the scale shown in Figure 3.11. You may recall that the normal scale classifies customers under five headings:

■ Very satisfied

■ Satisfied

■ Mildly satisfied

■ Dissatisfied

■ Very dissatisfied

And move it to:

■ Completely satisfied

■ Very satisfied

■ Satisfied

■ Mildly satisfied

■ Dissatisfied

To move the scale upwards, you omit in your tally of 'satisfied customers' those at level 3 who have described themselves as 'satisfied.' To be counted as satisfied, customers must go a step further: They have to declare themselves 'very satisfied' or 'completely satisfied.' I recommend this to world class companies. They should accept only the completely and very satisfied as a definition of satisfaction. How does this work in practice? At

Disney, taking only those top two levels into account yielded a satisfaction rating of 82 percent. Including 'the satisfied' yielded 99.3 percent! Two reasons to move the scale up:

1   There is more motivation for more improvement if you still have 18 points to go rather than 0.7 percent.

2   World class companies have an image not just of being the best but also, unfortunately, of being dinosaurs. So customers who are merely 'satisfied' will have a significantly different behavior to those who consider themselves 'very' or 'completely' satisfied. A company like 3M not only targets such a high score, it wants 50 percent to be completely satisfied and 50 percent to recommend the company strongly.

For 'normal' companies, a survey that yields two positive ratings, one middle rating and two negative ratings will provide enough information to start making improvements . As far as comparisons are concerned, I find that, as a rule of thumb, in business-to-business when you are below a 95 percent satisfaction level (using just the top two levels) you are not a world class operation. When you are below 90 percent you are in trouble. For customer services, when you are at 90 percent or above you are in the world class category, but if you fall below 80 percent you are beyond hope, trying to replace lost customers by pouring advertising into a bucket riddled with holes.

Increasingly countries such as Sweden, Germany, the US, and Japan have introduced national barometers that give scores by industry for comparison. Unfortunately, except for Germany, the scores are in figures, such as 8.7, which makes comparison possible only if you employ the methodology in question. This might be mathematically correct but does not speak to anybody!

Having worked with over 100 companies on service quality measurement, I have often found that what is simple frequently becomes complicated. So here a few tips to summarize.

## Don'ts about measurements and service concept

1   Don't do a survey if you have few clients. Visit them one by one!

2   Don't rush into quantitative research if you don't understand customers in the first place. A focus is richer than 10 surveys.

3   Don't do surveys too often. It takes time to design a new service or to modify or improve current quality. It's better to spend the money on improvements than on measurements.

4  Don't express your promise in evasive or verbose terms. Make it sharp, concise, and measurable.

5  Don't express your standards in terms of procedures (how to do it) or tasks (what to do). The standard needs to ask 'why' – that is, what benefit there is to the customer. Eliminate tasks and procedures that do not deliver benefits to customers.

6  Don't forget that support and administration departments also have customers. They can provide value as well – even the financial controllers! Make this explicit.

7  Don't keep your standards of excellence secret. Use them in all training and coaching.

8  Don't make standards boring, or smother them in heavy manuals. Use image, visuals, and cartoons. Adapt your communication for your audience.

## Don'ts about measurement of deliverables

1  Don't keep your surveys a secret. Share the results as widely as possible, and use them to educate your staff on customer orientation.

2  Don't use meaningless data. A score of '4.33 average satisfaction' means little to the layperson. Instead, say, '50 percent completely satisfied, 20 percent very satisfied' and so on.

3  Don't use scales that speak to nobody. Why use a scale of 1–10 or 1–5 rather than adjectives (completely, very satisfied, agree, disagree, or yes/no!) Use visuals such as smileys when you share the results.

4  Don't use a 'balanced' scale (as many plus as minus signs) unless absolutely necessary, and certainly not when there are no minuses to be shown. If you want to make progress, it is better to learn more about the difference between the very satisfied and the completely satisfied.

5  Don't delegate completely qualitative and quantitative surveys to outside market research firms. Go to focus group discussions yourself: You might help the facilitator to tailor the questions more effectively if you are there to listen. Have your administration and support divisions – IT, accounting and so on – do some or all of the quantitative surveys. This will improve their feel for customers, and you will learn about the limitations of questionnaires.

# The 10 questions for measurement

1 Do you have a balanced measure of quality in reality as well as perceived by your customers?

2 Do you have balance or a 'scoreboard' between doing the job right tomorrow and doing it right today?

3 Do you know the relationship between customer satisfaction and profit?

4 Are your measurement results known throughout the company and known down to the front line?

5 Are they presented in an action-oriented way?

6 Are they presented in a motivating way?

7 Do you use your measurements (especially ghost shopper trials) in all your training programs, including induction?

8 Do you regularly benchmark against others (competitors or the like) to see where you stand?

9 Is there sufficient time between two measurements to allow correction?

10 Do you include in your measurements customers and non-customers (those who bought and those who did not buy)?

# The 10 questions for value delivery

1 What is your service concept – your USP?

2 Does it translate your value proposition(s) effectively?

3 Have you translated it into a commitment? A guarantee? Is it posted everywhere in your company?

4 Have you defined your levels of excellence?

5 Are they expressed in terms of customer benefits?

6 Are they known from every new member of your team?

7 Do they translate into service standards – that is, quality levels that are measurable?

**8** Do those service quality standards encompass all service encounters (physical, transactions, interactions)?

**9** Do you balance the physical, transaction, and interaction encounters in the design of your service levels, or do you put too much emphasis on one of the encounters?

**10** Do you put your money where your mouth is – that is, allocate resources properly across the three encounters?

# Managing customer complaints for profit

**Systems and processes** for the optimum handling of customer complaints are among the best investment opportunities available in customer service. Here are some reasons why:

- Building good relations with existing customers is all the more important in an economic climate where new customers are harder to acquire.
- Good complaint handling and recovery systems bring additional sales and improve the image of the company.
- Investments in good recovery systems have a ROI of between 50 percent and 400 percent – a figure rarely equaled by other investments.
- Complaints are 'free' information provided by customers which can help to improve the quality of service.

In spite of these facts, few companies make the investment necessary for an optimal complaints handling system. Customer service departments are often staffed by under-paid, under-qualified people. Frequently the view is that complaining customers are the enemy: 'They want something from us.' Often, complaints are not fed back completely or accurately into the organization so that improvements can be made. Nor are complaints used to update databases (when they exist) or alert marketing, sales, and operations to perceived problems. In the absence of feedback and information systems, angry or dissatisfied customers continue to be approached for more business by the marketing people, even though current problems remain unsolved. This makes them even more angry. Finally, most companies do not even know how many complaints have been received, since recording methods are often limited to formal, written or oral complaints, addressed to a specific department such as customer service. Little heed is paid to complaints made verbally to staff or distributors. Yet such complaints may outnumber the formal written ones by as much as a factor of 10. And compliments, which occur much more rarely, are not exploited to their full advantage. Usually, there are 10 complaints for every compliment, with exceptional companies reaching a ratio of four to one. Remember, compliments can be used to motivate teams, and as a source of customer bonding, where relationships are rebuilt through dialog.

As a result of all this, companies may lose heavily committed customers – those who take the time, effort and energy to complain – at a fast rate. In fact if you dig into the data, it is relatively easy and inexpensive to prevent those losses from occurring, and to transform your angry customers into ambassadors.

# Customers who complain are friends not enemies

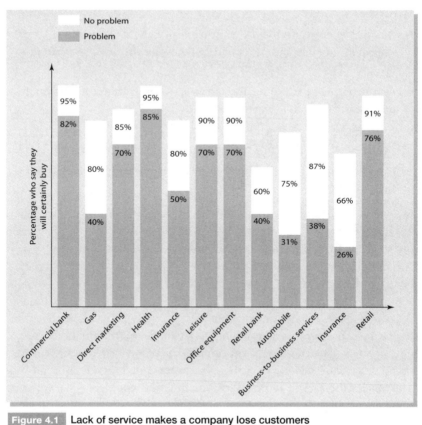

**Figure 4.1**    Lack of service makes a company lose customers

*Source: Data from TARP (Quality Progress, March 2000) /Jacques Horovitz Institute*

Of course, dissatisfied customers are less likely to buy again from the company than those who have had no problem. But, surprisingly, the rate varies quite considerably from industry to industry, as shown in Figure 4.1.

Very few unhappy customers actually lodge a complaint. Again, the ratio varies from sector to sector, as shown in Figure 4.2. However, customers usually prefer to go elsewhere or remain silent. There are several reasons for this. They believe that it is not their job to help correct a problem, or that their voices will be unheard. They may not want a confrontation. Or, quite simply, they just cannot be bothered to make the effort.

Customers who have a problem and complain are more likely to buy again from you than those who have a problem and don't. Even a customer who complains and doesn't get a response will re-purchase in 37 percent of cases. In contrast, only 9 percent of the uncomplaining customers will buy again. This suggests that customers who

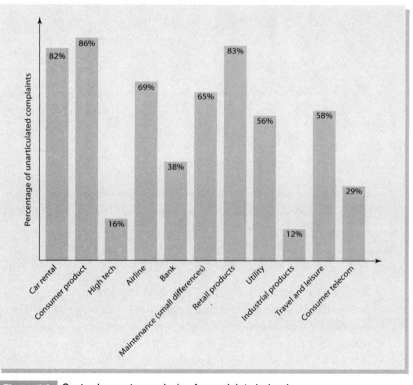

**Figure 4.2**    Sector-by-sector analysis of complaints lodged

*Source: Data from TARP (Quality Progress, March 2000)*

complain are, in fact, very loyal – particularly if they get a satisfactory
response. On average the loyalty of customers who complain is in the region
of 50 percent, as shown in Figure 4.3.

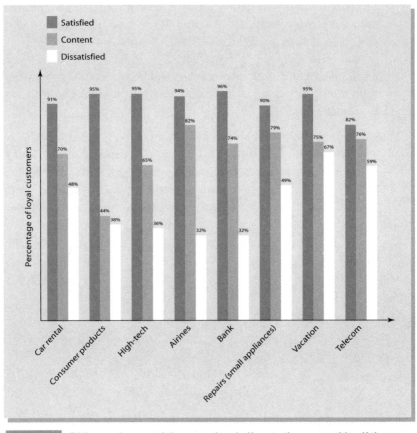

**Figure 4.3**   Of those who complain, more than half go to the competition if they are
dissatisfied with the response

*Source: Data from TARP (Quality Progress, March 2000) / Jacques Horovitz Institute*

Finally, it is unfortunately the case that most complaints get lost
within companies. These complaints are articulated at some level –
front line, supervision, regional management, dealer – but never
reach the customer relations department; so they are not recorded. In
fact only 1 out of 20 complaints reaches top management via the
customer relations department. The problem/complaint 'pyramid' is
depicted in Figure 4.4.

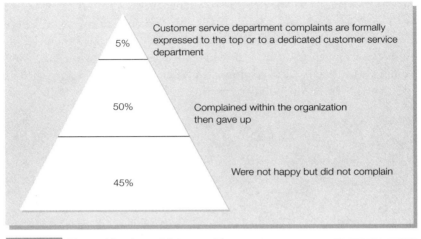

**Figure 4.4** The problem/complaint pyramid

It is interesting to note that the most of the complaints in the top 5 percent come, on average, from customers who have already complained twice about the same problem before formalizing the complaint in writing or by telephone. They may have complained first to their regular company contact, then to the contact's superior, to the distributor or to a factory manager, and still they insist on being heard.

When British Airways (BA) decided to revamp its customer service department, it found the following:

■ One-third of the customers were somewhat dissatisfied with BA.

■ Yet 69 percent of the dissatisfied customers did not register a complaint.

■ Only 23 percent of this group spoke to someone who worked for BA.

■ Only 8 percent finally filed a complaint to customer relations.

Furthermore, the airline noticed that 50 percent of the dissatisfied customers who did not complain left, while only 13 percent of complainers defected. As a result, BA computed its total loss of revenue from customer deflection, as shown in Figure 4.5.

BA acted on this information. For the 8 percent of customers who lodged formal complaints, the airline increased speed of response from 12 weeks to 5 days. For the 23 percent who spoke to a member of BA's staff, the company provided a more immediate response by giving employees additional authority to respond. BA set up listening posts to find out what the silent 69 percent was thinking. And the whole system paid back within a year – even with a 150 percent increase in the traffic of complaints (the 69 percent were no longer so silent). In addition, speed of response decreased the need for monetary compensation by 8 percent. All in all, £1 spent on managing complaints brought £2 in additional revenue. Not bad, considering that most costs in the airline industry are fixed.

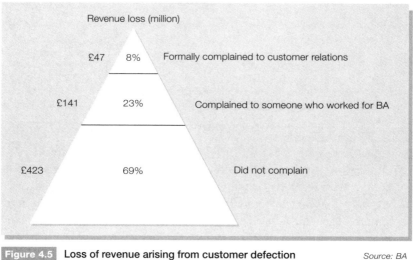

Revenue loss (million)

£47    8%    Formally complained to customer relations

£141    23%    Complained to someone who worked for BA

£423    69%    Did not complain

**Figure 4.5**  **Loss of revenue arising from customer defection**    *Source: BA*

# Your first priority: Respond immediately by empowering front line staff

The evidence presented in the previous section suggests that the greatest opportunity lies not with the persistent 5 percent who already make themselves heard, but with the 50 percent of customers who complain at some level within the organization and then give up. The best response system, therefore, is one where a customer's complaint is dealt with immediately and at the time of the first contact – the 'fix it now' approach, as Disney terms it. This requires all employees in contact with customers to use their initiative and be empowered to do so. When British Airways (BA) decided to revamp its customer service department in the late 1990s, it imposed the following: All employees are authorized to settle complaints up to a value of $5,000, and have a list of 12 gifts to choose from.

Empowering front line staff and distributors alike to recover immediately is a major project. A number of methods are used to achieve this goal.

## Full empowerment

GrandVision, a retail optical and photo processing company with 800 stores in 15 countries, declares as part of its 10 employee rights: 'You have the right to do whatever it takes to satisfy the customer without permission.' Companies often fret that such policies will result in abuse, bad judgment, and overspending from front line staff. In fact, I have found that, to get rid of a 'problem,' CEOs and senior executives will be more generous (sometimes too generous) than front line people dealing with customers every day. Front line people are quite reasonable; so are customers in their demands. Try it when there is little risk of abuse, which is the case for most industries.

## Limited empowerment with escalation

At FedEx, the customer service representative can spend up to $500 to find an immediate solution if a problem arises. For instance, the representative may send a cab to pick up a misplaced parcel or send incorrectly sorted data via the telecommunications system. Anything above that amount has to be authorized by a supervisor. At the Ritz Carlton hotel chain, the limit is $2,000. Cast members at Disney Hotels have a pre-determined list of things they can do, from awarding a free meal voucher to giving a present. Such policies apply best to larger companies with a high front line turnover.

## Full escalation

In many companies, the front line can do nothing. Banks are like that; you must ask for permission to reverse a charge made by the bank and reimburse the customer. Public services such as tax offices are similar. You will not get an immediate answer to an appeal for lower tax liability. In such cases it is important that there is someone at a higher level to whom the matter can be referred and who can make the necessary decision. It is also important that every front line employee knows such a person exists. In most department stores – which are neither a public service nor a bank – a complaint can lead to the following exchange:

'I am sorry, it's company policy.'

'Get me the supervisor.'

'I am sorry, the supervisor is not in this morning. Anyway, you don't have your receipt.'

Compare this dialog with Nordstrom's famous slogan, issued to employees: 'We will meet any unreasonable demands from our customers!' What a contrast. I went in once and asked a front line employee for a copy of their training manual. I got it.

# Service guarantee

This is another method companies use to ensure that, in event of problems, there is a response to alleviate the pain. It is quasi-automatic, and does not rely on judgment. To be successful, a service guarantee has to meet certain standards:

- It has to be extraordinary: something that tells your customer you mean it. Something that hurts if your service is poor, so that you will improve fast.
- It has to be meaningful to the customer – that is, the compensation should fit the mistake.
- It has to be easy for the customer to understand (no lawyer's jargon).
- It has to be easy to invoke: no witnesses needed, no receipt, no paperwork, no call for judges or lawyers.

The concept of a service being easy to invoke merits a little more discussion. Consider security, which could be defined as 'the protection of citizens.' As such it is a service provided by the state, and every citizen ought to be guaranteed such protection. Yet it is difficult to invoke. When your house has been burgled, you are made to feel like the criminal, not the victim. There are so many questions, so many forms to fill in. And, of course, insurance companies have understood that if you make it difficult for customers to claim, they will give up. If no forms are filled at the police station, no claims are made. Then claims decrease and so does crime. Easily manufactured statistics!

Finally, a service guarantee has to be unconditional: no fancy footnotes, no small, light grey type on the reverse side of the page, no separate conditions. Does this sound unrealistic? No, I have found many guarantees fulfilling those definitions. Here is one example: GrandOptical – a company that sells spectacles in one hour – offering a seven-point guarantee:

- If we don't make your glasses in one hour, we deliver them anywhere you want – free of charge.
- If you can't adapt to the glasses (in the case of progressive lenses, for example), we change or reimburse – whatever your choice – within 30 days.

- If you don't like them (possibly after your partner has seen them), we change or reimburse as you choose within 30 days.

- If you break them, we will replace them at no extra charge for the first 12 months and find an immediate replacement pair, if needed.

- If we don't have the model you want, wherever you may have seen it, we will get it for you in 48 hours. (In the beginning the competition would come into the shop and ask for one of their own models. GrandOptical would then buy it from them at retail price and sell it back for exactly that amount.)

- If you don't like any model we have, we will have one custom-made for you.

- Finally, if you find the same model cheaper somewhere else, we reimburse the difference.

Each of the seven points addresses a problem that a customer could have. Of course, a process manager has been appointed to oversee a reduction in problems in each of these areas. And the company is outpacing its competitors in annual growth.

Whatever method of empowerment you choose to rectify mistakes, solving problems on the spot remains the first priority. This means that you will have to train front line staff to listen and provide an appropriate personalized response. Usually a minimum of two days' training on handling complaints on the spot, accompanied by the appropriate role-playing, will achieve the objective.

## Your second priority: make more customers complain

The 45 percent of customers in the pyramid who were unhappy but did not complain will probably increase their business – with your competitors. These, and the 50 percent who complained once and then gave up, must be motivated to air their grievances. The most obvious first step is to ensure that customers know where to address complaints. Make the procedure as easy as possible. For this, you need to create listening posts.

In one major restaurant chain, the name and address of the CEO is printed on every napkin. And if the communication channel is well publicized, with many people using it, the next step is to ensure that they feel listened to, understood, and see action as a result. The Mandarin Hotel chain, for example, abandoned a system of measuring customer satisfaction with a questionnaire in favor of a direct approach. Now employees take the initiative in engaging with guests in order to solve problems on the spot.

Another example: GE opened a call center for all its customers. For each $10 the company spent, it got $17 worth of new business back as a direct result of answering questions and resolving customer problems. Dell Computer takes the initiative to call all customers four months after a purchase (500,000 calls per year). Not only does the company solve problems, it transforms dissatisfied customers into ambassadors for Dell and its products.

In 1995, Disney introduced the 'five interactions per day' program for all its cast members. This means that everyone in the parks and hotels is urged to engage in five interactions with five different customers. Employees were surprised to get mostly positive interactions and compliments, and were able to spot problems immediately.

## Your third priority: delight the five percent who make a formal complaint

On average, people who lodge a formal complaint have already made two attempts to be heard before finally sending a letter or phoning the customer relations department. They really want to continue doing business with the company: hence their persistence in trying to help solve what is, or is perceived to be, the problem. They require an even faster and more personalized response than the other 95 percent. By 'fast' I mean: 24 hours for a call center to deal with a telephone complaint; 24 hours to post a written acknowledgement of a complaint; one week should be the norm for responding to complaints received by mail.

Ritz Carlton has a rule called the 24/48/30. It means 24 hours to acknowledge, 48 hours to assume responsibility, and 30 days to solve.

As for personalization, the secret is to understand that not all complainers in the top 5 percent category have the same expectations. (For that matter, neither do the remaining 95 percent.) In our studies with clients, we have found that customers who finally get in touch with a customer relations department fall into one of five categories:

1   Quality controllers (about 2–30 percent)

2   Reasoners (about 20–25 percent)

3   Negotiators (about 30–40 percent)

**4** Victims (about 15–20 percent)

**5** Fans (about 5–20 percent).

Although proportions vary, it is important to realize that, beyond a simple understanding and observation of tone, vocabulary, mannerisms and – with face-to-face encounters – non-verbal behavior, each type of customer expects a different response. Quality controllers want to tell you what is going wrong so that you can improve for their next visit or buy. Negotiators want compensation for perceived damage. Victims want empathy, reasoners want answers to their questions, and fans want their congratulations to circulate – they would like to become involved in a fan club.

Failure to recognize this segmentation leads customer relation departments to frustrate complaining customers. And this is very common. Of the many leading European companies we surveyed, none furnished a customer satisfaction rate above 50 percent on the response to complaints. In simple terms, every second response from the customer relations department fails to satisfy a customer who takes the trouble to express displeasure on at least three occasions. In written answers to complaints, most companies use standard paragraphs assembled on a computer, creating a 'mass-customized' response. This method seldom employs the type of segmentation described above, and fails to provide the personalized approach needed.

Let's look at one type of complainer – the quality controller. If this person is really to be delighted ('delight' signifying the extent to which the customer's expectations are exceeded), the response should not merely describe the quality improvement measures being taken. Since it is hardly possible for the improvements to be implemented by the time the complaint is answered, a follow-up letter should be sent some months later to confirm that the problem has indeed been resolved. For an even greater measure of delight the follow-up letter could include an invitation to participate in a customer focus group, a panel, or a visit to the premises to witness the changes made. That would be a real treat!

Another type of complainer is the victim. To achieve delight, what is needed first is empathy to show your understanding of the situation. Then a gesture that generates emotion is called for. Let's say that a mother contacts Disney, explaining that she booked a stay of three days and nights with her five-year-old. Unfortunately, after one day the child fell sick, and had to be taken to a hospital nearby. Having safely returned home, the mother writes about how helpful the Disney employees were in taking the child to hospital. (The best response on the spot would have been a visit by a Disney character to the hospital; the worst would have been a voucher.) Disney replies with a postcard signed by Minnie and Mickey Mouse and a personal touch. This delights the mother and child even more, even leading to a second thank you letter.

Such a personalized approach requires a heavy investment in training customer relations staff, and in information technology. At British Airways, customer relations personnel have a four-week training program. At KAO Corporation, the Japanese cosmetic/household product company, all customer relations representatives are university graduates and have a three-month training program, which includes selling the products in stores. Information technology should enable staff to answer most questions from customers on the spot. BA's customer care system involved an initial investment of about $5 million. Each staff member has two screens, one showing the complaint letter, the other displaying retrieval options. Information on customer records, the reservation system, and the operating systems is available on-screen. At KAO each representative has three screens. A retrieval system provides information about current products, advertising, distribution (the where, what, how questions), a second screen gives menus, while a third screen provides answers to the 'why' questions.

KAO's training provides two types of knowledge:

1   Products/services/corporate structure.

2   Ways to handle customers face-to-face, by phone and by mail.

Training for giving answers includes listening skills and communication skills, using the retrieval systems, and adjusting to the different categories of complainer likely to be encountered.

# To inquire about a complaint or not to inquire? That is NOT the question

A key issue related to training is the inquiry. Should you inquire before answering a customer's formal complaint? Yes – definitely. But the purpose of the inquiry should not be to ask whether the customer was right or wrong. You should discover what is currently being done to solve the problem or to answer the customer's questions.

In a study made for a major tour operator, we found that, following every complaint, an inquiry was made. It involved questioning the resort, the travel agent, the air carrier, the booking office, and so on. All in all, it took from two to four weeks to get an answer to the following question: 'Was the customer right or wrong?' Not how the company was going to solve its customer problem, but what was 'objectively' right or wrong with the customer's complaint! The total cost of those useless inquiries was 100 times greater than all the free vouchers awarded to dissatisfied customers – which naturally the company never recouped. Such waste! It created disorganization in the resorts, inflicted paperwork on the travel agencies, and annoyed the reservation center. So when dealing with the 5 percent of people who take the extra effort to lodge a formal complaint, consider that the customer is always right. It is a matter of perception. As for the tour operator's customers, a survey found that only 47 percent of those who complained were satisfied or very satisfied with the response, and 58 percent doubted they would ever go back!

# A goldmine of free information

The customer service department can be a goldmine of qualitative and quantitative information, if the data it generates are properly fed back into the system. In addition, all departments (manufacturing, R&D, logistics, and so on) should help the customer interface to provide good answers, especially to questions from the quality controllers and reasoners among the complaining customers.

KAO, mentioned above, has an online system updated daily with information on products, service, advertising and promotion, and other issues. Its customer service department of about 10 people answers 40,000 inquiries annually. Furthermore there are 150 online displays in other departments – R&D, marketing, production, and sales – which provide information about current complaints and inquiries, as well as input for managerial presentations on the quantity and handling of complaints. This is a remarkably fast and efficient way to transmit information from the customer to the appropriate part of the company so that something can be done. Heavy users, possibly early adopters, also provide rapid feedback to companies. Renault surveys cab drivers on car quality, since these drivers cover as many kilometers in six months as a normal driver would travel in four years. The same goes for the software industry, where companies like Microsoft supply beta versions to developers in order to uncover bugs quickly.

## Compliments from customers: good for motivating employees

Compliments are, of course, much rarer than complaints. Customers are more likely to say what is wrong rather than what is right: the ratio of compliments to complaints is about 1:10. However, there are exceptions. World class companies like Disney receive one compliment for every three complaints; at Singapore Airlines the ratio is one in four. As channels of communication open up and responses improve, the number of compliments will increase. Not only do compliments deserve an appropriate response, they are excellent people motivators. When a compliment comes in, top management should go direct to the employees responsible for the product or service praised, and tell them so. This may compensate for any lack of positive reinforcement from the employees' immediate superiors – or supplement it, where it exists.

## Managing compliments: bravo for the thank you and thank you for the bravos

This is the title of a little booklet – 100 pages thick, full of customers' compliments – that was offered to every single employee of a hotel chain to thank them for having received so many compliments over the whole year. Of course, this booklet was made possible only because there were compliments from clients! Otherwise it would not have been 100 pages long!

So the first way to manage compliments is to get lots of them. A world class company will receive up to 10 compliments for one complaint or problem. In order to receive a lot of compliments, a company needs to:

- Be extremely good – compliments are not expressed as easily as complaints. The service has to be extraordinary to be noticeable and expressed by customers.

- The softer 'emotional' part of the encounters between the customer and the service provider has to be aroused: i.e. the five senses (physical encounters) and the interactions. Do not expect compliments merely by being good at executing a transaction. Nobody is going to compliment you for delivering the parcel on time. You will get one if, when it rains, the driver puts a plastic cover over the parcel with a note saying 'Sorry, it may not be aesthetic, but it will protect it from the rain,' or by bringing it to your doorstep a hundred meters away!

- Compliments should be forwarded immediately to those who deserve them. They should be recognized in public, and reinforced by compliments from management. There is a virtuous circle in compliments: a positive comment that leads to more excellent service that leads to more compliments.

## Customer insults

From the above heading you might think that this section is about customers insulting the service provider because they are ill mannered, in a society where social norms are disappearing!

In fact, it is the other way around! This is about the bad customer service representative who is rude. I am talking about procedures that aggravate strained relationships or create a bad one. A recent article in the *Wall Street Journal* (2003) mentions the increased irritation of customers who become the victims of company procedures supposed to maximize risk control to the detriment of most customers who are not at risk at all.

We are talking here about a deliberate attempt by a company to issue new policies that will make existing customers feel badly treated, despite the fact that they have been good customers in the past.

Let me give an example. Everyone knows that merchandise gets stolen in a store. Two attitudes are possible:

■ Prevention: take the risk into account in your pricing, put a sign up declaring that thieves will be prosecuted, and employ a security guard and alarm system. In this way you do not penalize 'good' customers.

■ Inspection: train all your staff to spot thieves, put the merchandise under lock and key, and tell your staff their job is to protect the merchandise rather than help the customers buy. All are punished, all become potential criminals! As a result, the good customers feel it is an insult to them:

■ They think the service provider is punishing them.

■ They think it shows a lack of appreciation for their past business.

■ They think it demonstrates a complete lack of knowledge of customers.

Visa has either a new CEO or CFO who has decided to reduce fraud – an admirable objective. But of the many ways of doing this, Visa has chosen to block a customer's card, without notice, if the expense patterns are 'abnormal.' This is what happened to me. I decided to buy five airline tickets for my family holiday, because I got a good price for the tickets. Visa stopped the deal at three tickets, not allowing me to buy the other two until I called them to discuss it. Why? Because buying five tickets from the same airline seemed abnormal to their computer. I've been a high value customer for a long time, but I have to call them if I want to make a high purchase – this is profitable for them, so you'd think they'd want me to spend my money!

A similar thing happened recently with my Swisscom cellphone line. Swisscom cut me off because I had forgotten to pay my May bill – although I had paid June, July, and August, and the previous 96 bills over eight years in good time. I paid the bill once I realized my mistake, but then received a call telling me I had four days to pay, and should send a fax to prove it. I couldn't fax any proof, because I had paid the bill by bank transfer! The gist of the response was, 'If you do not send proof within two days we will cut the line because we will not look at the account to see if you have paid.' One wonders how they can identify so quickly that I have not paid, to call me and tell me so, while being unable to see on the same account when I *have* paid.

In general, the reason for customer insults is simple – the rules are there for the minority who abuse the system, and they end up punishing the innocent majority. Yes, businesses are open to abuse, but why spend so much energy protecting against those abuses to the detriment of customers who could be highly profitable for you? A rule biased toward risk is bound to reduce customer service. A bank will send a reminder to a loyal customer to show that he has gone overdrawn. But when does the bank send you a letter to say, 'Your current account has a lot of money in it and has had for some time, so here are some options for higher interest accounts'? Never – although my bank statements explicitly say that I have an 'account manager.' What do account managers do all day? The system raises a flag to say when an account is overdrawn. Why not raise a flag when a current account reaches a certain amount of credit, so that the account manager can write to you discussing better ways of putting your money to work?

But no – the bank only contacts you when you default. What a way to insult customers and never increase business!

Apparently the different components of an organization do not talk to each other enough to align their objectives. Lawyers and accountants protect their company. Marketers sell the earth and operations people get slapped!

Take the example of the Air France ++ card. It tells you that you are privileged, and thanks you for spending so much money with the company. Then you go to the counter and arrive two minutes late (28 minutes before take-off instead of 30) and get ticked off! And while they're telling you off, you notice that the plane is not even announced for boarding yet – it's delayed, but no one has said for how long. What is the point in having a VIP card if they are going to treat you like this? The marketing department creates beautiful little pieces of plastic designed to recognize loyalty – and the operators punish you for it.

I rented a car for my family to drive from New York to Boston. I wanted to visit Boston, then go directly back to Geneva. AVIS was the service provider – their familiar motto is 'We try harder'. After driving for four hours, I dropped the children at the hotel and asked the concierge where the nearest AVIS return center was. He told me the street, and showed me where it was on the map. I parked the car and walked the whole length of the street hoping to find the elusive center, with no success.

The AVIS rental agreement offered a toll-free assistance number. So I called it – to see how much harder AVIS would really try.

'Hello, I am in X street trying to locate your center and cannot find it. Can you tell me where it is in the street or whether I have the wrong address.'

'What is your contract number?'.

'I do not see what my contract number has to do with your address.'

'Sir, I need your contract number.'

'Here it is – 889 62362562221.'

'Just a moment, please. What are you doing in Boston? According to your contract, you must return your car in New York!'

'I took the car in New York to drop it off in Boston. But that is not the issue. Can you tell me where your garage is?'

'Sir, you must return your car in New York otherwise we will consider it as a stolen car!'

'I am not returning the car in New York. I am staying in Boston. This is not your problem. Just give me the address.'

'But it is our problem. You need to go back to New York.'

'You must be joking. Are you going to give me that address, God damn it? If there is a problem, when I return it here, they will tell me!'

'Sir, you should calm down and be polite. Your contract says back in New York, that's it!'

I hung up. I went to the only underground garage in the street and – miracle – once inside, I saw an AVIS sign, hidden from the street. I left the car, gave the contract number and asked if everything was okay. And it was!

Again the example shows that the procedure is designed to avoid losses rather than help the customer. As a result all customers become suspicious.

# Impact of insulting good customers is dreadful

The big argument I got on Visa is 'But don't you want to feel protected?' My response is: They already charge an extra fee for the version of the card which includes an insurance! Insults will result in disloyalty, either immediate or deferred (it takes time to change all your credit cards)! It leaves customers one common ground on which to evaluate alternatives: price! And in cases such as those described above, word of mouth is negative, destroying all the efforts of advertising designed to demonstrate how good the service is.

# Getting started

- Begin by assessing how many dissatisfied customers you have in reality; how many complaints you receive; how and where they are expressed (channels, frequency, volume, purpose, mode of expression, type of response).

- Evaluate globally and by segment how satisfied your complaining customers are with the present response mechanisms (assuming they get a response). Assess the subsequent buying behavior of (a) those who get a response and (b) those who don't complain or get a response.

- Look at the systems currently in place for answering complaints, getting feedback and costs. Also look at the empowerment system.

- Evaluate the potential gain of a good response. Remember you can get between 170 percent and 400 percent ROI. How many extra customers will keep buying as a result of good complaint handling?

- Design a new system that includes the organization, training, staffing profile, first contact 'fix-it' programs, and IT infrastructure. Compare the costs with benefits in terms of customer loyalty, increased purchasing, cross selling and so on, as shown in Table 4.1.

- Set up an action plan to:
    - open up channels of communication;
    - react immediately;
    - improve internal feedback by communicating complaints quickly;
    - answer fast and appropriately in a cost-effective manner;
    - measure results in increased feedback from customers, increased satisfaction with answers, and increased sales. Turn angry customers into ambassadors to improve the reputation of the company.

**Table 4.1** Analysis of customers who complain to a major car manufacturer

| | |
|---|---|
| Customers who complain formally | Are brand loyal |
| | ■ On average have bought into the brand for 13 years |
| | ■ Have had 4 cars |
| Where do they complain? | Wherever they can: dealers, region, customer service, marketing, CEO |
| What do they expect? | 1. Consideration |
| | 2. A concrete solution |
| | 3. Speed of result |
| What do they get? | 73 percent dissatisfied with response |
| What do they do? | ■ 14 percent will change brand within 12 months |
| | ■ 40 percent intend to do the same |
| | ■ Will speak to 32 people about their problems |
| What does the car manufacturer lose? | ■ 4 percent of sales |
| | ■ Annual profit contribution lost: 8 million euros |
| What does it cost to fix it? | 1 million euros |
| Payback | Less than 2 months |

# Don'ts

**1** Don't staff your customer relations department with frustrated employees who have been moved from somewhere else in the company.

**2** Don't put your listening post near the washrooms where nobody notices it (seen at a Wal-Mart store).

**3** Don't underinvest in direct problem-solving on the spot by all front line staff.

**4** Don't underestimate the capacity of your field people to both please the customer and defend the company's interests.

**5** Don't continue to woo your dissatisfied customers for more purchases until you have solved their current problem.

**6** Don't see complaints handling simply as a matter of replying to people who have written to you or your official customer relations department. After all, a customer is free to choose his channels and process – not yours.

7   Don't answer with disjointed, computer-generated paragraphs.

8   In case of compensation, don't assume the customer wants the shirt off your back. Ask what is expected of you. The customer might be more reasonable than you.

# The 10 customer complaint questions

1   Do you know how many customers are dissatisfied? How many voice their dissatisfaction, and how many don't? Do you know the profile of complaining customers and their current purchases?

2   Do you have this information for all possible channels of communication?

3   Do you know how good your current system is at transforming dissatisfied customers into ambassadors? Alternatively, how many leave because of your system?

4   Do you have a staff-empowerment system to solve most problems as they arise?

5   Are you sure you have enough visible encouraging listening posts to encourage dissatisfied customers to voice their satisfaction and express their complaints?

6   Is your customer relations department considered a profit center? Can it transform angry customers into positive relationships? Or is it just a cost center, where what counts is productivity?

7   Are customer complaints acknowledged within 24 hours and properly answered within one week?

8   Are your internal feedback mechanisms for problems detected by customers spread widely enough throughout the company to allow speedy cross-functional corrective action?

9   Do you customize your answers according to the type of customer who voices dissatisfaction?

10   Have you recently started new procedures that punish customers because of a few black sheep? Beware – customers will feel insulted soon!

# 5

# Loyalty building

**Sometimes giving satisfaction** is often not enough to ensure that customers come back. There are many reasons for customers leaving. Some can be acted upon, whereas others lie outside your company's control (for example, a simple change of address may take away 10 to 20 percent of customers every year!).

Here are some of the main reasons that can be acted upon:

- 'It was okay, but not great or compelling.'
- 'It was good but so much more expensive; it was not worth it.'
- 'I got a killer offer from another vendor that I could not refuse.'
- 'I was curious to see how others did it.'
- 'Even if I liked it, it's always better not to have all your eggs in one basket.' (Banks say that of their customers.)
- 'Everybody else was buying elsewhere.'
- 'It was great until I was assigned a new account manager.'

## Is it worth keeping customers?

It is possible to do something about the reasons outlined above – assuming that your company is convinced it is worth the effort. So, is it?

Yes – if two conditions are met:

- You know the cost of attracting a new customer compared with that of retaining an existing one.
- You know the value of keeping a customer (that is, profitability over time).

## Cost of attracting new customers *vs* keeping existing ones

Most studies show that attracting new customers is indeed more expensive than keeping existing ones. The costs include:

- Communications, promotion, selling.
- Making a proposal (cost is time).
- Cost of setting up to deliver well on the promise the first time(s).
- Mistakes made in serving the customer the first time, and costs of correcting them.

These costs have to be compared with the expense of keeping existing customers:

- Cost of maintaining the relationship (including time, communication).
- Cost of special treatments and conditions from a lunch to a discount, to decreased price to keep the contract.

Which is cheaper? Each company has to assess it on its own position rather than relying on generalized estimates or rules of thumb.

Consider Elis, a leading European linen rental company. To get a new customer, such as a hospital or restaurant chain, it needs to take the time to study the customer just to make the bid. It needs to make the clothes, linen and uniforms bespoke, to meet the customer's specifications including, for example, a company logo. It must take an inventory before making the first delivery, set up the information system that will tell it (and the customer) the linen consumption in order to optimize delivery rotation, and more. Elis has calculated that all these costs are recovered only if the customer stays with the company for three to five years. Only then will it start to make money.

Or take the consultant who needs to make a proposal (requiring a pre-proposal analysis), possibly underestimating the time needed to deliver the initial stages, convince management to buy, and set up a team. Most consulting companies will tell you that in the first year of work with a new customer, they lose money. They make money in the second and third years, but lose again in the fourth year, unless they do new work for the same client.

Have you worked out these costs? Generic studies show that it costs between 25 and 400 percent more to attract new customers than to keep existing ones. Therefore an increase of 5 percent in the rate of retention can increase profits disproportionately, by as much as 75 percent. This analysis, of course, assumes that your current customers are profitable – that is, that their life-time value (revenues realized by them over their lifetime, minus costs needed to keep them) is positive.

If it is worth your while to keep your customers (or there is no alternative, as happens when location is the key determinant of customer attraction), investigate the causes of customer disaffection in greater detail to find solutions.

# The right question: how to serve customers profitably. Not the wrong question: how to get rid of unprofitable customers

The reason for keeping customers is the value they bring to us. However, we are sometimes too fast in eliminating unprofitable customers rather than serving them all profitably.

You often hear senior executives and consultants pompously asserting that 'We have to get rid of unprofitable customers.' It sounds professional! It even could sound gutsy. In fact, many big consulting firms make it a selling point in their pitch: Our fees will be recovered by getting rid of your unprof-itable customers! Board members even praise their new CEO for backing such a rational approach to restore profitability!

In fact, it is one of the most damaging sentences for a company, for several reasons:

■ When it reaches the front line, where distinctions between 'unprofitable' and 'profitable' customers are difficult to make, all customers become the enemy. Operators may start to think 'we treat them too nicely. We do not get enough in return for what we give them. They abuse us.' So all customers end up being treated as if they are unprofitable.

■ At management level, the easy approach is to get rid of a problem that was create by… management itself. Who attracted the customers in the first place? Us. Who promised them the earth? Us. Who spent thousands in advertising to make them believe we were so great? Us. What a waste! Could we not have thought it through in the first place? Cellphone operators attract customers with priceplans, free handsets etc., and then discover that some people buy the service just to get the handset from a particular promotion – and then continue to use the competitor's service! Or take the example of certain banks in Brazil and Argentina, which write off debts rather than work on a way of getting the country back on track. The same thing has been witnessed in Japan, with banks writing off corporate debt. It's bizarre but absolutely true that some senior managers and consultants prefer to get rid of a problem they have created – rather than solve it. This is topsy-turvy management practice.

■ The third reason why we should not try to get rid of unprofitable customers is one of definition – how do we decide who is profitable and who is not? Cash positive or cash negative would be a better measurement than 'profit.' Post-Enron, we could consider cash to be a fact, and profit to be an opinion! Should we allocate full cost per customer, as banks do? If so, what happens when a customer leaves? Can we reduce our fixed costs – or will they have to be allocated to other customers? Are we talking about past profits or future potential profits? All these issues mean that we need to know where customers fit into the chart in Figure 5.1.

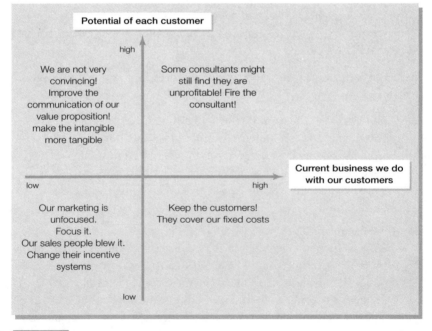

Figure 5.1    Customer potential value

Do we know how to assess potential lifetime value? Do we know how the cost of doing business will evolve if we work harder? When is the unprofitable customer going to become profitable?

▪ Finally, is our database clean enough not to confuse account profitability with customer profitability? Most telephone operators know their customer only by their account details. The same goes for banks and insurance companies. One account may be 'unprofitable,' and immediate action by the 'wise businessman' could result in the customer closing the account – and any other accounts held with the same company. So what are the right questions to ask?

▪ Did we target well enough to avoid customers we cannot serve profitably?

▪ For those customers we have retained, can we serve them profitably? Can we rethink our customer service processes in such a way that we stay profitable for those customers, or that customer segment? Provided, of course, that the way we measure profitability per segment and the customer is reasonable in the first place.

The first question leads to the following issues:

▪ Communication and positioning: Are we tight enough in our advertising/visuals/text to say who we are for?

▪ Do we have enough selective criteria for our sales people, call center or other order system to refuse, delay, or discourage customers we cannot serve profitably through price, long lead-time, or lack of attention?

The second question – serving profitably – leads us to reinvest our service processes in light of what we can afford to spend. It usually ends up being one or several of the following trade-offs:

▪ More or less *intensity* of service depending on the value of the customer to us.

▪ We provide the service or the customer provides it *himself* (or part of it) depending on its size or potential.

▪ Service at a *distance* or face-to-face.

▪ In-house staffing and resources to serve some customers or outsourced and variable costs for others.

A few examples might help illustrate the above trade-offs:

▪ Should a customer with low usage of his cellphone or bank account receive a bill as often and as detailed as one who is a heavy user?

- Should the customer himself find out how much he has in his account or should the bank tell him?

- Is there value in sending an agent once a year to renew a single low premium contract, or only when there are several contracts due for renewal?

- Should we outsource a call center for insurance assistance or have it inhouse?

The above trade-offs are the easy ones. And in most cases, they allow us to reduce our costs while more or less keeping intact the value to the customer.

What can be more exciting and rewarding is to completely rethink our service delivery process in such a way that it not only helps us serve our different customers or customer segments profitably, but also increases services to all customers.

Most hotels compute their cost per department such as accommodation/food and beverage/telephone/bar and mini-bar and ancillary services (photo-copying, concierge, etc.), and charge customers for each. Couldn't they be incorporated in one all inclusive price in such a way that the company can reduce its costs while, at the same time, giving the customer more value? This is what Châteauform – a French hotel specializing in hosting business events – has done for its corporate clients. One price *includes everything*. As a result, no check-in or check-out is necessary, there are no credit card costs, no mini bills of 1 euro for mineral water, one photocopy of a page, no staff cost for barmen, and no accountants checking the bills. And for the customer there is no time wasted checking in or checking out, and checking the bill. There is more fun to be had helping yourself at the bar (also included). The hotel's profits are 10 points (points being a percentage of profit contribution of a sale) higher than rival hotels in the same category.

# Why do you want them to come back?

As well as evaluating whether it's worth enticing customers back, it is essential to set some objectives in the event of their return. What do you want the returned customer to do?

- Buy more of the same? How big is their appetite? There must be a limit. Do you know it?

- Buy other things (called cross-selling although it should be called cross-buying) because they do not need or want more of the same, but something different. Do you have something else which is palatable for which you are a legitimate supplier in the eyes of your existing customers?

■ Bring other customers with them who will buy. Do you promote positive word of mouth?

■ Buy more often – in that case what will influence the frequency of buying? Do you have an impact on it?

■ Only continue to buy from you. A defensive move against a tough competitor may be necessary.

■ Buy all their needs for that particular service/product from you rather than spreading their purchases over several suppliers. What will make them switch? Do you reassure them?

Set clear targets for what you want the customer loyalty to achieve. This will help greatly when choosing the right kind of loyalty scheme and what type of communications you need.

Some loyalty schemes work in certain conditions better than others. Some are more adapted to certain types of products and services than others. Successful loyalty schemes involve one or several of the following:

■ Values: People are loyal to companies or organizations that share the same values as they do.

■ Self-esteem: People are loyal to companies or organizations that help them reinforce their self-esteem.

■ Constant contact: People are appreciative of companies or organizations that keep in touch (at the right moment and for the right reason).

■ Recognition: People are loyal to companies that recognize and appreciate their business.

■ Reward: People stay loyal as they get rewarded for it.

■ Involvement: People stay with a company or organization if they feel they can participate in the development and betterment of their supplier, from which they can also benefit.

These characteristics are depicted in Figure 5.2.

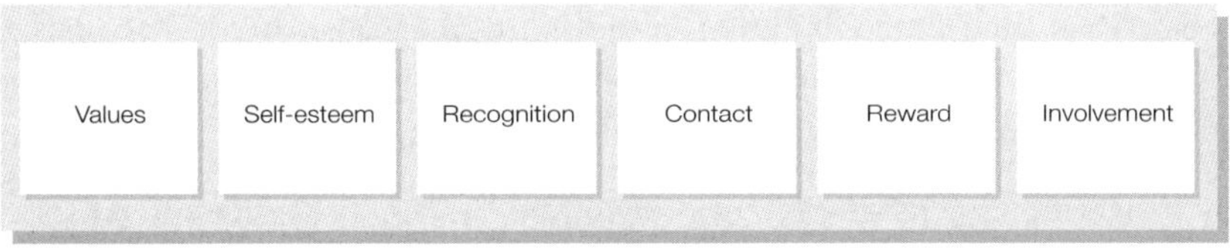

| Values | Self-esteem | Recognition | Contact | Reward | Involvement |
|---|---|---|---|---|---|

**Figure 5.2** Different types of loyalty schemes

## Loyalty through values

This scheme can be particularly useful for products/services that make people think about current problems in society. The Body Shop promotes natural products that are not tested on animals. For people against animal testing, this represents a bond that can lead to loyalty.

Benetton has played a lot with leveraging humanitarian values ('United Colors of Benetton'), and forcing debate on important issues (such as racism or AIDS). It has promoted non-utilitarian and existential values. Not only have those campaigns achieved above average recognition (76 percent compared with 44 percent for standard comparative brands) and above average attribution (67 percent compared with 19 percent for standard brands), but they also have a good average positive response (56 percent compared with 60 percent for standard brand). In addition, Benetton's sales multiplied by a factor of 10 between 1986 and 1995.

The reinforcement of loyalty through values is, of course, achieved through the brand, and its key expression is advertising. In addition, visible proof of the values defended must be present: photography of the factory manufacturing the product, description of the products to show how natural they are, etc. PR campaigns can reinforce such loyalty building schemes. When Virgin Atlantic was set up, with values pertaining to the underdog trying to attack the dinosaur, Richard Branson used every possible event to get press attention and say how poor British Airways was, charging so much for so little value!

## Loyalty through self-esteem

This scheme effectively address reasons for leaving such as:

- 'I am not sure of the value.'
- 'Why is everybody else buying somewhere else?'
- 'It was okay but not great.'

Here, customers have not been completely reassured that they have made the right choice. They remain unconvinced. If this applies to your product or service, then image building is the solution. A great brand becomes a great buy! A known brand is a booster of self-esteem: 'If everybody knows who I buy from, then I must be right.'

Self-esteem happens when a customer buys a product or service and is proud of it! Self-esteem can mean 'I am somebody' or 'My friends recognize me as somebody' or 'I have achieved something.' It is a statement about yourself. And the brand can reinforce such psychological needs. In fact, a good brand is a booster of self-esteem as long as it conveys the right message. Leroy Merlin, a do-it-yourself store chain based in France, has cleverly pledged on self-esteem in its recent advertising. It shows people talking about the house they live in. Those houses are original, innovative, and personalized. The slogan is about 'making your dreams come true.' A clever way to say both that at Leroy Merlin we can help you build your house, and also that people who buy from us are original and innovative!

Young & Rubicam identify four key pillars upon which brands are built. These are summarized in Figure 5.3. Each pillar in turn relates to one of two key attributes: vitality or stature. Whereas vitality might be more important for stimulating buying, stature is definitely more important for building loyalty. And it can become the best lever to increase loyalty. It means that communication on the brand must be addressed to current customers as much as to new customers to succeed in striking a balance between 'I want to join' and 'It was definitely for me.'

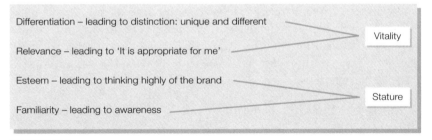

Differentiation – leading to distinction: unique and different

Relevance – leading to 'It is appropriate for me'

Vitality

Esteem – leading to thinking highly of the brand

Familiarity – leading to awareness

Stature

**Figure 5.3**  **Pillars on which brands are built**

The brand must be reinforced through visible proofs. The slogan and everyday consistency of brand communications reinforce self-esteem. If I want to buy some sunglasses, for example, it's the staff member attending me who creates the visible proof of the brand. What the salesperson should not do is say that the sunglasses look great. The salesperson should say that *I* look great when I am wearing them. You look like Brad Pitt, they might say – or Demi Moore, depending on what sex you are!

It can also be reinforced through 'club' activities such as the one that Harley Davidson organize each year in California where riders ride together to enjoy togetherness and show each other their motorcycles.

The first two examples of loyalty-building schemes – representing values and self-esteem – rely heavily on branding and advertising. In advertising, it is often said that everybody knows that 50 percent of the money spent achieves useful results. The trouble is, that nobody knows which half it is. I would add that, of the 50 percent for which we know something, at least half – if not more – is used to raise or sustain the self-esteem of those who bought to a level at which they want to buy again and tell their friends. (So much for using advertising for traffic building.) Why do Armani customers buy more from Armani? Because their friends know the brand. It is cool, chic, modern, and fashionable.

In fact, if we move beyond products to services, the impact of advertising and branding is probably even more important for loyalty building than for attracting new customers. The reason is that, as was mentioned in Chapter 1, when you sell a product you need to make the tangible intangible. This means adding psychological or emotional benefits to an otherwise non-differentiated product. Here, the brand and its character can make a difference.

When you sell a service you make the intangible tangible and convince your customers not only that you have a good service but also that you have the ability to serve. Here, advertising is less effective: Information, testimonials, word of mouth, and peripheral cues are more effective. In fact, when I did a survey for the vacation industry about why people chose a particular desti-nation and service provider, less than 15 percent said it was advertising. Over 70 percent said it was their friends!

On the other hand, the brand can reinforce loyalty by enhancing self-esteem.

## Loyalty through contacts

As obsessed as companies are about CRM, data warehousing, data mining, and other data overload mechanisms, they forget the simplest way to reinforce loyalty – to *stay in touch*! Granted, it takes some effort to stay in touch proactively. You want to avoid being seen as too intensive or too overwhelming, especially if you propose something a customer does not want.

However, there is one very simple series of contacts that can do a lot for loyalty: those that are initiated by the customer! Because he has a problem, he meets your truck driver or your repair man. This is a very good oppor-tunity to discuss, to get inputs, to inform the customer about your new developments or your new service offer. Do the company representatives feel it is part of their job to 'resell the company', 'reassure' about the choice made by the customer, 'reassess' his needs, 'rethink' modes of doing business, and 'refresh' the memory of the customer about what we can do for him?

In order for contacts to be meaningful they must rely on one or two sources.

▥ *Customer generated contacts*: Where can they happen, when can they happen? Are we prepared – do we take the opportunity to know more about the customer and use the opportunity to reinforce bonding?

▥ *Company induced contacts*: When is the right moment? What is the right occasion? What do we say? What do we try to learn?

## Loyalty through recognition

Recognition is a very old way of building loyalty. In our grandparents' stores, in small villages, the grocer or butcher recognized all customers by name, and remembered to suggest a product a particular customer liked or round down a price for loyal customers.

In a world of mass markets and mass encounters, companies now try to recreate on a large scale the personalized nature of those transactions by employing new techniques of customer recognition. In itself recognition can be enough keep a customer loyal. Contrast two restaurants. In the first, the maitre d' comes to greet you by name, takes you to your favorite table, immediately bringing that San Pellegrino water you like; then he tells you and your friends of a specialty you will like. In the second place, they ask you to spell your name to check whether you have a reservation, and shout to the waiter 'Party of four,' having asked, of course, how many of you there are, and not who you are. No contest!

Too many companies jump on the bandwagon of points, discounts, free miles and the like in order to reward loyalty – we shall discuss these in the next section – without knowing whether the customer in front of them is new, occasional, a heavy purchaser, or came yesterday. Photo Service, a French one-hour photo development retail chain, made this mistake and it cost them about 15 percent of sales. The company created a card that customers could purchase for 18 euros. This loyalty card gave them a free film plus a 12 percent discount each time the customer had a film developed. After a very detailed, careful analysis, Photo Service discovered:

▥ The cost of free films and the 12 percent discount came to 15 percent of sales.

▥ Good customers felt it was not enough in return for having 10–12 films processed ever year.

▓ Occasional users (5–10 films) did not care and did not renew.

The cash registers could not read the card. A simple device on the card or cash register or both would have revealed the last time the customer came to the store, and what he or she had developed. It would have made for a much more appropriate recognition system.

Are your customers recognized when they come to see you again? Do they feel recognized? When they have a problem, do they have to repeat the complaint each time they meet a different contact person? If they have a problem, do you send them a generic, glossy mailing piece singing the praises of the product or service that gave them grief? Although a customer has failed 10 times to respond to a particular invitation, do you continue to send generic information or do you try to find out what would be of interest? The list goes on.

Recognition can be reinforced for the customer through several means:

▓ A simple acknowledgement that you know the person.

▓ Something personalized 'just for them.'

▓ Something that reminds them of their last interaction with the service provider.

▓ Something that helps them use your service even better (a tip or an extra document).

▓ Something that simply thanks the customer for doing business again.

▓ Personal attention.

▓ Something that is proactively proposed that perfectly matches their evolving needs!

Amazon.com is a good example of a loyalty scheme using recognition (and for that matter, they are also good at rewards and customer involvement). They use a profile system to build up knowledge of what interests a particular customer so as (proactively) to send more of the same, i.e. authors or books the customer might like.

Recognition is often enough to make customers loyal because in today's impersonal, indifferent world it makes them feel special. So don't jump too fast to implement the rewards scheme that managers without imagination use, thinking that 'bribing' the customer is the thing to do. It's more expensive and is by no means certain to work – even if it is fast and practicable.

## Loyalty through rewards, or how to avoid discounts

In certain circumstances, a company will need a reward / incentive system to supplement its recognition program or keep its customers. Those circumstances are many, and include:

▨ Competitive threat: Others are doing it.

▨ Pressure on price: Give better value instead of additional discount.

▨ Preventing a newcomer from entering a market.

▨ Incentives needed to keep distribution loyal.

▨ Perceived high price of the brand.

▨ Desire to compile databases on customers and frequent buyers.

In these cases the reward can be an effective tool to prevent customers migrating.

Surrounded as we are by points, miles, loyalty cards and membership cards (these days an average customer has three to five loyalty cards in his wallet), I wonder whether the approach really works. One estimate suggests that 25 percent of loyalty cardholders are ready to switch to another card if it has better benefits (Mori study).

Often it is too late to ask the question. If your competitors have gone down this route, you must follow, just to stay in the game. It is part of the cost of doing business. And this expense involves not just the rewards but the administration, staff training and hotline, plus IT costs. However, for companies that have not yet started or are still in a position to reorient their choice, here are some criteria that may help plot a direction that truly increases loyalty rather than dishing out discounts without furnishing real proof that customers will stay loyal.

▨ **Target customers:** It is better to select the customers for whom you wish to do something special. It could be that they have shown loyalty or represent high value. Much better to focus than to include everyone as a member of your loyalty scheme. A good scheme distinguishes between the loyal customers you want to reward and non-loyal bargain hunters.

▨ **Offer choice:** Rewards that can be redeemed (to claim a wide variety of products/services) appeal more to the customer than a mere cash discount, or greater use of your own product/service. That is why airlines have created partnerships with other vendors permitting miles to be used for other services. (At some point customers need to land and do something else.)

■ **Rewards must be aspirational**: The largest chain of discount supermarkets in Canada (60 percent market share) is very selective about the presents gifts it offers as rewards in its catalog. Wal-Mart and French hypermarkets have started optical stores not merely because the optical market is attractive, but also because getting spectacles with points accumulated from buying canned food and toilet paper is more aspirational than getting more toilet paper for free.

■ **High probability of getting the reward**: Both the purchase frequency and the level of reward will determine in the mind of the customer whether the probability of getting a reward is worth the effort to buy again.

■ **Ease of use**: Rewards which require the customer to keep scores and tallies, or go through a special channel rather than the usual one, are less appealing. The same can be said of rewards that apply only in certain periods (when customers don't want to fly, or in school time when they cannot take the family, for instance). Likewise, schemes that force the customer to present a 12-digit membership number to claim a reward at, say, a rental car station are less alluring. Therefore computation and redemption processes, as well as timing of use, are critical.

■ **Club effect**: Even such dry rewards as vouchers or coupons or points are better received if they are wrapped in a 'club feeling,' with some intangible attached. This is where recognition and rewards work best together. These soft privileges can include a special hotline, advanced or exclusive information, special events (as implemented by Harley Davidson, for example) and special recognition. Customers who receive their points often say: 'We are told we are special but we don't feel special.' According to one estimate, 40 percent of the effectiveness of corporate communication to loyalty cardholders is lost when the customers come into contact with staff.

■ **Rewards that support your value proposition and its image**: Any reward that supports your value is more likely to be appealing than a reward that is just a discount. For instance, a Porsche loyalty card purchased at £75 also ties the customer in with Mastercard, Lufthansa and Visa. However, more importantly, the scheme allows members to leave their cars at the Avis lot free if flying Lufthansa business class. The car will be kept securely and washed for free while the customer travels.

Pro 7 is a German TV station. For £30, the customer gets club membership, free subscription to a TV guide, and a VIP service linked to the channel. The service includes tickets for live shows, backstage passes to shows and movie shoots, meetings with favorite stars, trips to movie locations around the world, and job opportunities as an extra in TV shows. All these are part of the reward. The Ikea family club membership includes insurance, plus access to a databank where families around the world can exchange houses for holidays.

▦ **Updates**: Interest in a loyalty program diminishes after a few years. Updates, added benefits and changes are crucial to keeping interest high. Porsche has added rental of bikes, ski racks, ski boxes, service delivery and pick up of cars at the customer's address for maintenance over the years to its loyalty scheme.

▦ **Reward segmentation**: A good reward system will be more attractive when its target is homogeneous. Within the same company, different schemes may apply to different segments. A cellphone service provider may find that business customers want free minutes, free access fees, and no long-term contract without discounts and information. The individual consumer on the other hand might prefer a free cellular upgrade when new technology is developed, free minutes from home, and battery renewal. Airwave has catered to both private users and corporate accounts accordingly and has reduced the current nightmare of all mobile phone operators – churn rates – by 30 percent.

▦ **Regular communication**: This helps build a relationship as well as promote the rewards. Fidelid, a French consulting company that specializes in loyalty programs, carried out an interesting study in the fashion field. It showed that frequent communication with customers led to more and more frequent purchases although, judged on a one-off basis, individual direct mail pieces did not seem effective when compared with the reaction of a control group. An invitation to a show did not translate into lots of people coming; a special package for Fathers' Day did not yield a lot of sales. However, the fact that customers were communicated to often yielded higher sales. Regular communication is indeed an important part of any reward system.

### Paying for the loyalty card

Following the question of who should be eligible for membership of a rewards scheme comes another issue: Should the membership be free or involve a fee? Paying membership involves a commitment on both sides. For the customer it implies an interest in the benefits; for the company it implies a commitment to deliver superior benefits.

In the USA Club Med started its Expert Program for its travel agents. To be eligible for the club, they had to sell a minimum number of 'bed–weeks.' They would receive special benefits such as automatic refilling of racks with brochures, a direct mail campaign to selected target customers around their agency, frequent information on their performance, staff training, a special hotline and booking call center. Most of these benefits, however, were not free: Window displays, mailings, and training were paid for by travel agents. After one year, the top sellers' loyalty had moved from 32 percent to 50 percent, signifying an increase of more than a third in the stability of its distribution.

GROHE, a German manufacturer of bathroom taps, has set up a reward/loyalty scheme which costs £85. Some 1,500 master craftworkers have joined in five years. They get marketing consultations, a magazine, a hotline and VIP treatment at trade shows.

GrandOptical sells its loyalty card at 40 euros. The benefits are 10 percent discount on future purchases, three-year insurance for breakages (compared with one year for new members), and a free magazine four times a year, which features special offers, invitations to fashion shows, etc. Within two years of enrolling, it appears that members buy more often (every 1.4 years compared with 2.5 years for rival companies), buy more (30 percent higher receipts) and bring more family members (1.3 compared with 1.2). So, all in all, charging customers for a loyalty card is feasible. It discourages pure bargain hunters. Of course, the benefits of paying must be readily perceived as positive.

### Rewards that are adapted to your business

To select the best reward system, I have found it useful to classify businesses according to two dimensions – frequency of transaction and intensity of relationship – giving four types of possible reward, depicted in Figure 5.4.

If the relationship with the customer is not intense, but merely involves simple, frequent transactions (banks, airline offices, or supermarkets), then points that can be exchanged for travel or merchandise will yield the best results. In 1995 Tesco, the British supermarket chain, launched its Clubcard loyalty program. Every pound spent yields one point. Every three months, cardholders receive a statement with vouchers and a magazine. Tesco has 10 million cardholders, and 50 million vouchers have been redeemed for merchandise. Even better is the Harvest Partners program of the American Cyanamid Corporation (ACC), launched in 1993. Every time growers buy, they get points. They can redeem these points with their dealers, and are

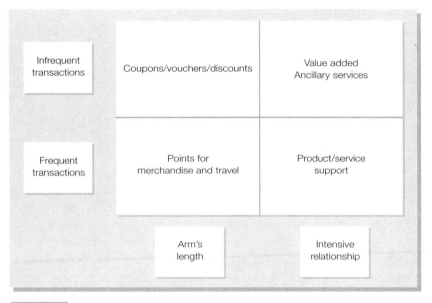

**Figure 5.4**   **Four possible types of reward**

offered special members-only promotions for trips, merchandise, saving bonds, scholarships, donations to community service projects, and added value benefits such as fishing trips and active wear. A database allows ACC to segment customers, track purchase history, target communication, allocate benefits, and measure effectiveness. It also helps dealers and sales representatives get a handle on who their most valuable customers are.

If the transaction is not so frequent, it is better to give a discount coupon that can be used to buy more of your merchandise. GrandOptical's card gives a 10 percent reduction for families who buy glasses. For more intensive relationships (a high involvement purchase such as a car or software), rewards will be different. They can take the form of product/service support benefits if the transaction is frequent (a free car wash or car servicing) or ancillary value-added services for less frequent transactions. For example, Microsoft UK's Advantage loyalty scheme gives 30,000 small office subscribers and 5,040 home office subscribers a magazine every other month, with hints and tips, for an annual fee of £35; for £95 it offers free training and a hotline. Microsoft's cardholders have generated 111 percent more revenue than others have. In 1997, IBM launched the owner privileges loyalty program. This provides support services, additional discounts on accessories and software, protection, e-mail updates, free software downloads etc. It is a co-branding effort with retailers selling IBM's Aptiva

PC. Every quarter, members receive coupon packs that can be redeemed at the stores of six retail sponsors: Best Buy, Current City, Computer City, Office Max, Radio Shack, and CompUSA. Membership costs $100 a year or $20 without a hotline. The annual renewal fee is $20.

## Customer involvement or commitment

Beyond outstanding service, another way to create and foster loyalty is to involve the customer in your business, or even include them in some joint activities.

Here are two examples of such involvement. For 1-800-flowers.com, a telephone and Internet based flower ordering company, floral design, decorating, care and handling, and seasonal tips add to the convenience of online delivery and contests. These make it an easy and value-added buy. In addition, the company offers a gift registry that allows customers to register up to 50 special occasions. Five days before the occasion, the company sends customers an e-mail to ask if they would like to buy a gift. It has found that they buy two or three times more often and spend approximately $10–12 more on each purchase. Games and buying centers for early holiday delivery also promote repeat order and tie-in rewards.

The FedEx website allows customers to track their own packages. 20,000 customers use it. They can create their own shipping form, arrange a courier, and more. Involvement can go even further. At Motorola, for instance, customers are involved in the recruitment of the sales force. After all, since they are going to be involved with those sales people for a long time, they might as well pick them in the first place! A retail group called Pinky invites all its customers to an event in its stores once a year, and uses the day to get feedback on its service.

Involvement is best exemplified in partnerships – that is, in formalized relationships where suppliers and customers work together on problems. Cebal does packaging for the food industry. Its graphics department helps the food manufacturer find the best design for the package in terms of appeal and attractiveness. Baumarkt, a German do-it-yourself store chain worked with its suppliers to change the logistics chain. Now, instead of insisting that all suppliers deliver to all stores, the company allows them to deliver to a central warehouse. It saves costs and adds service in the store, as the sales staff are not busy filling the shelves during the day; instead they can help customers buy.

# Which loyalty scheme to choose?

Since we have seen that four types of loyalty-building scheme are possible – self-esteem, recognition, rewards, involvement – the question is: Which will work best in a given situation? Notwithstanding competitive pressures that might force you to do as the others have done, I have found the table illustrated in Figure 5.5 useful in making a decision on loyalty schemes.

| Type of buy \ Type of motive to buy | Rational buy | Emotional buy |
|---|---|---|
| Transactions (or discrete buys) | Reward/contacts | Self-esteem |
| Continuous relationship (or frequent buys) | Recognition/contacts | Involvement |

**Figure 5.5**  Grid of factors to be considered when deciding on a loyalty scheme

If the basis of the relationship is a number of individual transactions, infrequent (or frequent with no requirements for follow-up in between), then rewards or self-esteem benefits work best. Rewards will work better for rational buys (low-involvement purchases based on information) whereas self-esteem enhancement will work better for more emotional purchases (high involvement purchase, e.g. an ego-boosting buy based more on credibility, word of mouth, and trial than on information).

For continuous relationships, where purchasers are frequent buyers or there is a need for follow-up, recognition or involvement will work better. Again this depends on the type of buy.

# From transactions to relationships: managing customer relationships

No matter what type of inducement is chosen for sponsoring loyalty, if customers are to come back they need to get a 'point of relationship' – that is, a communications link with the company to solve problems and buy more services. The company also needs this linkage to communicate its 'incentive' news.

Most companies have a 'yes–no' approach to prioritizing relationships with customers. Large accounts will have an account manager, small accounts nothing. Significant customers will get a hotline, less significant customers will be advised to read the instruction manual or visit the website. Wealthy customers will be met by a banker, others by the cashier or the ATM. Big accounts will be visited by sales people. Small ones will be sent a mailshot.

There is, of course, a link between the set-up costs of the relationship, its running costs, and its return. On the return side, it is better to calculate not what customers bring today but what they can bring over time (the so called 'life-time value'). This can give another perspective on the investments and expenses we are willing to put into the relationship system. On the costs/or investment side there is a whole array of possible set-ups which can provide a gradual approach rather than an all or nothing solution.

USAA has 5 million customers to whom it provides extensive insurance and financial service. At the core of the customer loyalty scheme is ECHO (Every Contract Has Opportunities), a system that captures any customer's query, complaint or compliment while the customer is talking to a USAA representative. The company gets 2,000 calls a week. Although the customer mostly induces this relationship, it provides an opportunity to propose additional services. Thus a car insurance claim is an opportunity to propose comprehensive travel insurance. It equates to the third step in Figure 5.6.

A study made by the American Society for Quality Control in 1996 showed that the main reason why customers quit was employee indifference (68 percent). This was followed, but at some remove, by product quality (14 percent), and then by competition (9 percent). This shows the power of the relationship, even if it is maintained only through an annual visit or a welcome call.

As shown in Figure 5.6, for many transactions, mail outs or emails are a useful communications tool. In 2000, e-mail accounted for 50 percent of all direct marketing sales in the USA.

Of course, the type of relationship management employed is linked to costs. But not only to costs. The frequency of buy also influences the preferred mode of communication. Figure 5.7 illustrates different types of service based on the frequency of service usage and the type of transactions, and Figure 5.8 identifies which relationship management is likely to pay off more, depending on the type of service.

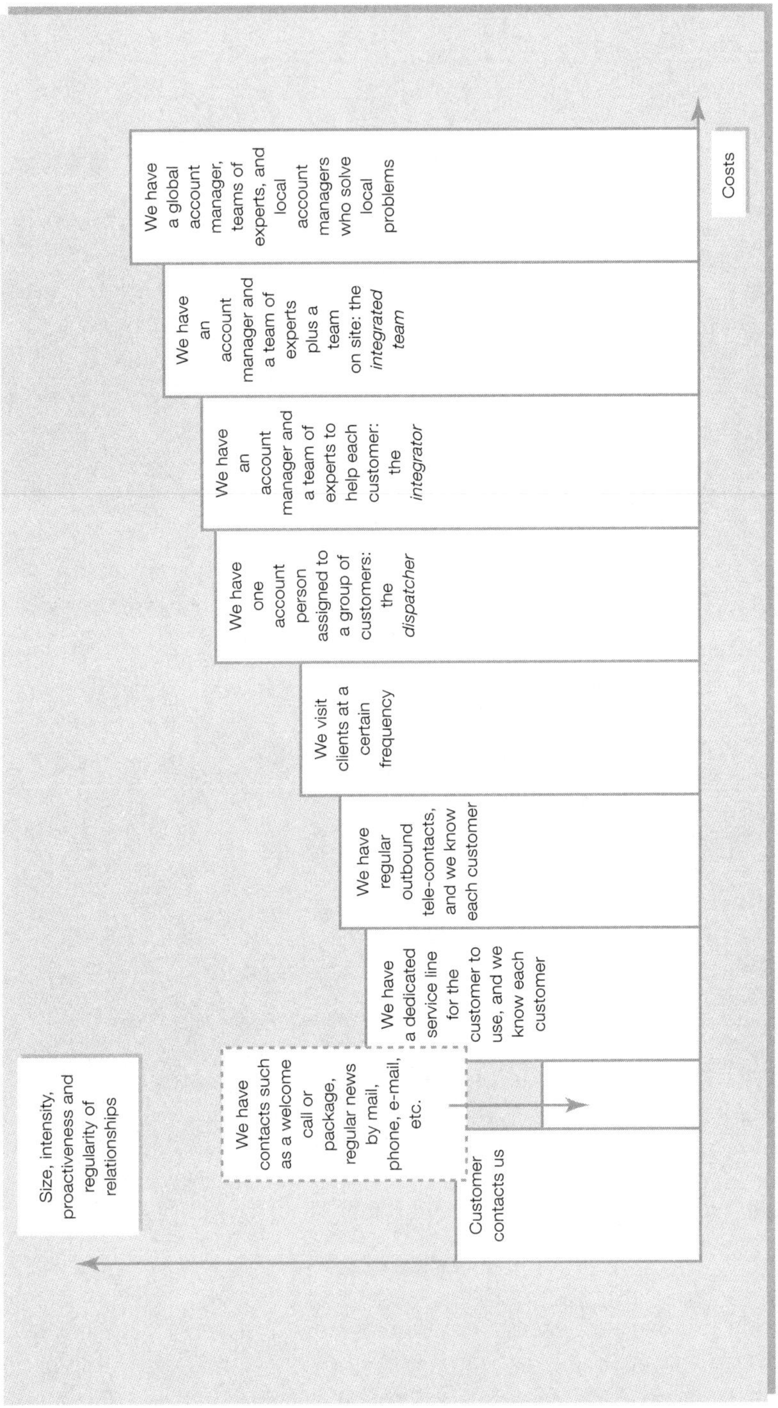

**Figure 5.6** Costs and benefits of relationship management

Size, intensity, proactiveness and regularity of relationships

Costs

We have contacts such as a welcome call or package, regular news by mail, phone, e-mail, etc.

Customer contacts us

We have a dedicated service line for the customer to use, and we know each customer

We have regular outbound tele-contacts, and we know each customer

We visit clients at a certain frequency

We have one account person assigned to a group of customers: the *dispatcher*

We have an account manager and a team of experts to help each customer: the *integrator*

We have an account manager and a team of experts plus a team on site: the *integrated team*

We have a global account manager, teams of experts, and local account managers who solve local problems

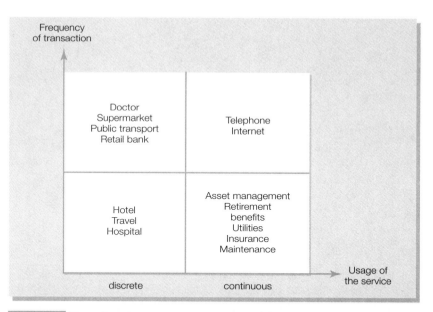

**Figure 5.7**  Examples of types of service based on frequency of transactions and usage intensity (business-to-consumer)

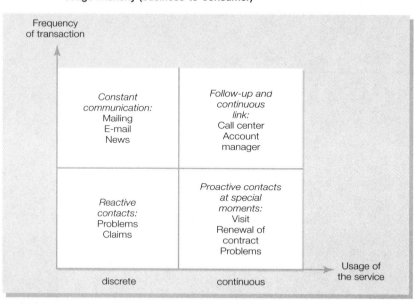

**Figure 5.8**  Types of relationship per type of service

Relationship management is a significant way of fostering loyalty: a global study carried out by Deloitte Research on loyalty in manufacturing in 35 countries showed the following relative impacts of different factors on loyalty (Figure 5.9). However, to be effective, relationships have to encompass the full virtuous circle, as shown in Figure 5.10. This virtuous circle must be accompanied by the proper means to maintain that relationship at all levels of the customer organization, with all the contact points.

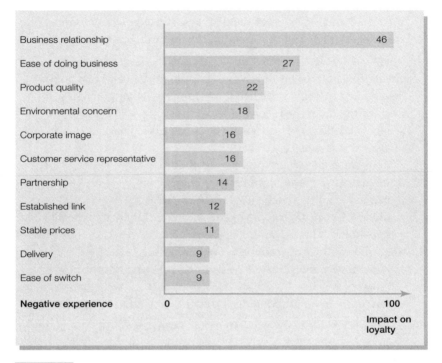

**Figure 5.9**   Factors affecting loyalty in the manufacturing industry

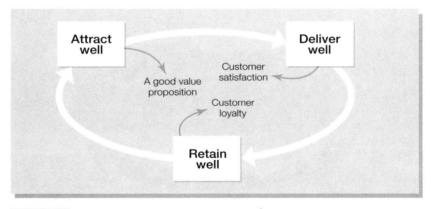

**Figure 5.10**   The virtuous circle of relationships

# Using the Internet to reinforce the customer relationship virtuous circle

Two established facts about the Internet:

1 It will not replace the old economy. Most experts estimate that only between 3 and 8 percent of the total amount of goods and services to consumers will be sold through the Internet in the foreseeable future.

2 It will mostly work for selling products and services under certain circumstances: thus selectivity is of great importance when choosing merchandise to sell on the net. Everything else being equal, it will work better under the following conditions:
   - more *information* based searches by customers rather than experience/credence searches;
   - more *standardized* products/services;
   - higher *margin* products or better services;
   - current *access* to merchandise is difficult;
   - order *size/value* high compared to shipping/fulfillment costs;
   - *convenience* is key – learning is easy;
   - *alternative* 'brick' distribution is not appealing;
   - immediate *gratification/five senses* is less important in the buying process;
   - *investment* in brand-building and traffic generation is minimal.

However, it is also becoming clear that the Internet can do a lot to reinforce links with customers. In fact, if we reconsider the virtuous circle of customer relationships presented earlier and illustrated in Figure 5.11, the Internet can have a positive impact on all aspects of the customer relationship, even if nothing is sold via the web.

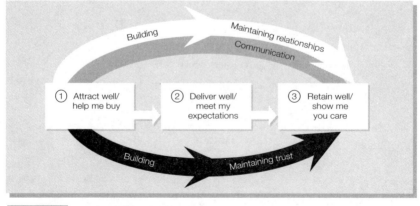

 **Figure 5.11** Customer relationships

Taking the impact of the Internet at each stage of the relationship, it becomes obvious that it can help the customer buy, contribute to his satisfaction, and recognize his loyalty:

▦ **Attract well**/help me buy: information/decision making/education/ reduce FUDs (fears, uncertainties, doubts). The Internet can help customers obtain information on the product or service, use decision-making tools provided by the supplier to speed up or enlighten their own decision making, become educated online to be in a better position to choose, or obtain references of other customers he can contact to reduce his fears, uncertainties and doubts. Schindler, for instance, has been putting its elevator specifications and plans on the Internet to be used by architects so that they can readily include them in their own plans and specifications when they present them to the authorities and contractors for bidding.

▦ **Deliver well**/meet my expectations: Internet technology contributes to satisfying customers, from online tracking of parcels, to online bank statements, to customer satisfaction surveys online, to online assistance and documentation.

▦ **Retain well**/show me you care: This can be in the form of personalized offers, affinity clubs, previews of new products/services, privilege services or special offers to loyal customers, frequent updates, and online information. These are some of the great benefits of the Internet that help create better relationships.

## Measuring loyalty

What is your loyalty rate? How do you measure it? Let us suppose that last year you had 1,000 customers. And this year the company's performance has been so good, you have 1,200 customers. When you look at those 1,200, it appears that 600 have bought goods or services from your company before and come back for more. Would you say that your loyalty rate is 50 percent? Not so great, is it? Now suppose you take a five-year base and for each year work out which customers came back from previous years. The results are shown in Figure 5.12.

Of the 600 customers who used your company five years ago, 400 have returned. At 66 percent this is better than the current year's 50 percent. Of the 800 who used your company in $t$–3, almost 70 percent have already returned within four years, and so on. Over the last three years (let us exclude $t$–5 and $t$–4, because we don't have data) on average 63 percent of

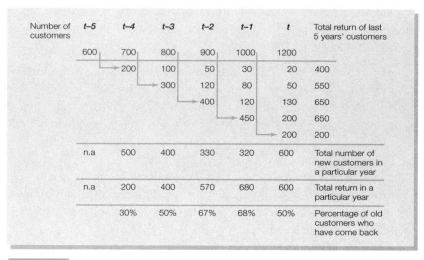

**Figure 5.12**   Measuring loyalty rate over time

customers will be seen to have returned if you also exclude from the calculations the 20 percent growth in customers in the current year. In other words, you use the $t$–1 level of customers instead of $t$ and find a loyalty rate of 60 percent (600 over 1,000, instead of 1,200). Loyalty is not about the percentage of customers in a particular year that have previously bought from you. It is about repeat buys. Loyalty is about the percentage of people who have in a particular time frame (e.g. one year, five years) bought once and repurchased. In a German insurance company, analysis revealed that, after 10 years, some 60 percent of customers left – that is, did not repurchase. (Nor were the policies in question life insurance!)

Such analysis requires a historical database, customer-by-customer, in order to obtain the pattern of repurchasing year-after-year, little-by-little. It can help target specific actions. For example, in Figure 5.12, on average, customers who started to buy in a particular year repurchased the following year at a varying rate. In $t$–4 it was 60 percent (300 over 500), whereas in $t$–3 it amounted to 100 percent (400 over 400). In $t$–2 it was 135 percent (450 over 330). So apparently the trend has been for more than one purchase the following year from an existing customer. However, in $t$ only 65 percent (200 over 320) of new $t$–1 customers have come back. Why? This is where a database that records dates of purchases (how recent) and frequency of purchase (and we could add monetary value) can help target specific action.

Beyond measuring how many customers return and how much they spend, it is also useful to know what we aimed for in the first place. What were our objectives? Was the purpose of creating loyalty to get our customers to:

- Buy more of the same?
- Buy more frequently?
- Bring other customers?
- Provide new business? That is, buy other products or services we sell (often referred to as 'cross-selling')

Measuring the contents of sales will tell you whether your communication and relationship approach was the correct one.

## Don'ts

1 Don't institute any loyalty initiative until you are sure that you have done everything you can about customer satisfaction, but are still losing customers.

2 Don't do anything unless you know why you lose customers: They might be dead, or have moved and so there might be no need.

3 Don't create a loyalty program unless you know your current loyalty rate.

4 Don't include everyone in your loyalty scheme. Target.

5 Don't favor disloyal customers through promotions.

6 Don't confuse repeat business with loyalty.

7 Don't rush into a rewards system. There are other methods.

8 Don't underestimate your database needs over time whilst pursuing loyalty programs.

9 Don't limit relationships to one staff member while abandoning all else.

10 Don't limit your calculation to current transactions, but look at life-time value.

## The 10 loyalty building questions

1 What is your current loyalty rate?

2 Does customer loyalty pay off for you?

3 How much can you gain if you increase loyalty?

4 Who do you target for loyalty building: All? Some? Which?

5   Which scheme – esteem, recognition, contact reward or involvement – would do best for you and your customers?

6   How effective are your current schemes?

7   If you choose value or esteem, how is your brand viewed?

8   If you choose recognition or contact, can you really recognize your customers?

9   If you choose involvement, how exclusive do you want to be?

10   How do you monitor success?

# 6

# Company structure and processes

**When efforts to improve** customer service fail, it is mostly for one reason: They are not fully integrated into the normal management processes of the company. Unless integrated, service will not be represented in the list of priority actions set for the company as a whole. One company that got it right is Xerox in the 1980s and 1990s. In 1983 it felt threatened by Canon and launched its first program of 'leadership through quality.' The initiative ran until 1987 when it was followed by a customer satisfaction program, still in action today. The first program emphasized doing things right: achieving zero defects, making efficient products, delivering speedier time to market, and new product introduction. The second emphasized customer service. It led to the launch in 1990 of a 'satisfied or satisfied' guarantee that allowed unhappy customers to change their photocopier. In tandem with this effort, Xerox embarked on a value extension program, moving from being a supplier of photocopying machines to its position as 'the document company.'

Fifteen years later (late 1990s), customer satisfaction was close to 100 percent (the goal set in 1987), return on assets was at 20 percent, and market share had been retained – even increased compared to the level at which it was in 1983. Xerox was also an early winner of the Malcolm Baldridge National Quality Award. This award was given by the US government to those companies which met a series of criteria for good quality work (in Europe, the equivalent is the European Quality Management Award). What is so striking about Xerox as a benchmark is the tenacity and the systematic approach it brought to bear on the issue. When one looks at Xerox and similar companies – Otis with its Service 2000 challenge, and Microsoft with its customer satisfaction program – it becomes obvious that defining and sustaining a long-term service strategy is not a one-off initiative. It's far more than a speech from the CEO, or a matter of measuring customer satisfaction or carrying out some other survey. To use a visual metaphor, a customer satisfaction strategy can be imagined as a set of interrelated management processes, like spokes, supporting a wheel that rolls service strategy forward (see Figure 6.1). The purpose of this chapter is to describe those elements.

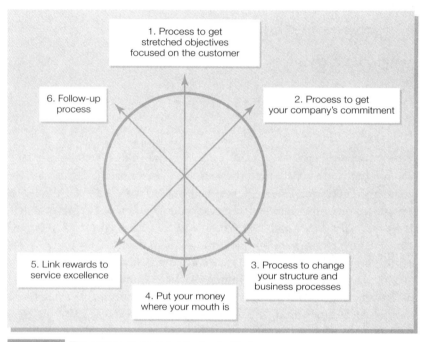

Figure 6.1    The service management wheel of fortune

Let's start by looking at the entire wheel, before going on to each element in turn. No element is independent. An *a la carte* approach whereby you choose item No. 5 and disregard others will not work. Success will come from a systematic, enduring, and balanced approach to all the elements.

# Stretched objectives focused on customers

To develop such objectives requires a good knowledge of customers, an ability to evaluate what could be gained through better service, and transforming the stakes into objectives.

## Know your customers

Does this sound trivial? It isn't. Consider companies with large numbers of customers, and consider the ease with which technology can help them build databases. Then consider the lack of detailed customer knowledge: It is appalling. Beyond simple demographics, not much is done. Disneyland Paris has over 1.5 million visitors coming to its hotels every year. At present, it doesn't capture or use this information. In many companies, most senior managers do not have regular contact with customers. Most marketing studies are filed away somewhere in the marketing department. Most segmentation is still based on pure demographics or SIC codes. Very few customers are ever asked for their opinion.

Many end-of-mission, end-of-project, or annual meetings with customers end up with the supplier talking rather listening in an attempt to justify why certain customer expectations were not met. Too few of the employees in regular contact with customers are ever asked what improvements or innovations customers would like. In fact, most companies cannot answer three simple questions:

■ How many customers (not cases, policies, tonnes, transactions) do you have?

■ What is your overall rate of satisfaction?

■ What is your loyalty rate?

Most companies do not ask friends or outside vendors to act as mystery shoppers – that is, pose as a customer to see what it feels like, and subsequently report back. Most employees – especially senior management – enjoy perks that give them customer privileges. They never experience what it feels like to be a real customer. They have products delivered to the office or go to a special outlet to buy; they may use a special pass, go to a special line or receive some other form of VIP treatment. Meanwhile, customers may receive a mailshot announcing marvelous new products or services while still awaiting a response to their latest complaint. Few customers get proposals that would help them spend more money with the company, simply because the company doesn't know what to offer them. How could it? It hasn't gathered enough information about them. There is little more to say on this topic; I urge you to return to Chapter 3 for advice on measurement if necessary.

Until your company has resolved this essential issue, you should not proceed to the second question.

## Know the stakes

Only when Xerox decided to have a single corporate objective – 100 percent customer satisfaction – did it achieve significant movement on this front.

Before 1987, the service goal was on an equal footing with return on assets and market share. It was not until top management appreciated a number of things about customer satisfaction that Xerox was able to embark on a fully-fledged improvement plan. The turning point was the realization that customer satisfaction (together with employee satisfaction) would lead to more sales (yielding greater volume with lower production and marketing costs) and increased productivity. These factors in turn would lead to more profit, hence a greater return on assets and thus on equity.

It is only when you know the relationship between service and profit, and that between service and customer satisfaction, that your company will be able to make real progress. Even with high technology products such as medical instrumentation, service may be more important than product. In this sector, surveys have rated product and service at 30 percent and 40 percent respectively. However, an increase in customer satisfaction may not always be your best lever for profit. In pharmaceuticals, speed to market can bring more profit than increased service to hospitals and doctors. In very high growth sectors, where innovation is the driving force, service does not come first. This is probably why Microsoft has felt the need for it only recently.

Knowing the stakes will help your company assess the investments involved, convert the bean counters to the cause of customer satisfaction, and reduce resistance. I once met with all the franchisees of Midas, a US repair chain for car tires and exhaust pipes, etc. I wanted to persuade them to proceed with a supervisor level of service and buy an educational/promotional list that would help them achieve it. They were convinced after I brought on stage two franchisees who had worked on a pilot project which improved sales and profit by 30 percent. So what is one additional point of customer satisfaction or service going to bring to you? Do you know?

## Stretched, extended and focused objectives

Declaring that 100 percent customer satisfaction was the goal Xerox set itself in 1987, invariably provokes a response from some people that this is impossible. People will insist that, among other things, there will always be one disgruntled customer. So let me clarify. The Xerox definition, '100 percent customer satisfaction,' includes customers who have said they are 'very satisfied' or 'satisfied' with the company (leaving room for more improvement, in terms of converting the satisfied to very satisfied). Second, it is better to aim for perfection and not reach it than to aim at imperfection and attain it. Third, I have often seen that companies have a better chance of achieving success in service when they choose ambitious objectives that stretch the company and its employees. Depending, of course, on how much is at stake, high or extended targets can be set for customer satisfaction, customer retention, attracting new customers to a new value, for reducing the number of lost customers, cutting the number of dissatisfied customers, cross-selling, and so on.

High targets oblige managers to discover new solutions, different solutions, and new ways. When the Zurich Group defined its new vision as 'simply world class, and a total solution for customers,' it forced the organization to stop thinking purely in terms of selling insurance products. It created a scope for merging life and non-life products into 'personal lines.' It pushed insurance out of mere risk avoidance, into providing solutions to problems. For example, if your house has been flooded, you need a new bed and a cleaner – not just a check.

As well as being ambitious, objectives have to be focused. Too often, there is an apparent contradiction or conflict between the customer-oriented objective and other corporate goals. And guess which ones win: financial goals, naturally. Returning to Xerox, one can see that by linking customer satisfaction to profit, management no longer had to express profit objectives. Profits came naturally – once the satisfaction targets were met.

Until 1985, at Club Med the *chef de village* (resort manager) had only one objective: to satisfy the customers. It was the basis for his reward. *Chefs* with the best score had the first choice for their next resort assignment. For the best practitioners, this was a good reason to celebrate; the top scores were celebrated in front of all, and held up as examples. It was the basis for promotion. And business was profitable – I cannot recall the profits being any higher since those days. In the mid-1980s, the management introduced the notion that *chefs de village* were also responsible for local sales and costs. Since then, with the possible exception of 1988 when a quality program was launched, customer satisfaction has been decreasing and, with it, profits. By blurring the focus, the company diluted its commitment to customer service. By making resort managers responsible for areas they were unfamiliar with, the company forced them to devote more of their time to new disciplines, and less to customers. With the new focus, the profile of these *chefs de village* changed. No longer were they the buccaneering type ready to celebrate a second Christmas, if the one on December 24th was not good enough. They became classic 'managers,' instead of tribe leaders; they were no longer so adept at creating an extraordinary experience for their teams and customers. An equilibrium was lost!

# Getting commitment

## Create the right mindset

It is not natural for people to be customer oriented. It is even less natural for their bosses to be so, given the constraints they work under. Organizations are measured by profit. Shareholder value is dominant, especially if a company is on the stock market. Financial analysts never ask about customers and satisfaction. Every week or month, reports from the financial controller's office emphasize data related to financial results, no matter how they were produced. Of course, almost every company was originally founded to meet some customer need. In the initial stages, the customer-centered mindset must have existed. When the company becomes successful, however, it starts to acquire administration and support personnel who do not share a fervor for customer service. As time goes by, new employees lacking the enthusiasm and energy of the pioneers join. As the organization grows, its flexibility diminishes, fuelling a relative indifference towards the original goals. This is accentuated by the requirements for short-term results from public companies.

There are two exceptions. The first is the company that has put the customer at the center of its ethos right from the start, creating and reinforcing a customer orientation by using its energies to create a culture of value for the customer. Classic examples are Starbucks, Nordstrom, Virgin, Kwik-Fit, and Singapore Airlines, all companies under strong leadership. The ethos might or might not survive the company's founder.

The second exception, which applies to most companies, is the crisis response: 'You move faster when you are kicked in the ass.' Xerox changed tack because Canon scared it. Otis prioritizes customer service because it now makes its money on service rather than on selling elevators. Microsoft is doing so because its quasi-monopoly status and arrogant image have provoked a legal challenge. British Airways did it because, once privatized, it was no longer protected by the state. FedEx re-emphasized customer service when DHL, UPS and others started to compete with it. SKF, the Swedish maker of ball bearings, did it when competition from the Far East jeopardized its profitability; it saw no scope for more cost cutting to stay competitive. Common to all these companies which need a 'philosophical transformation' is the requirement, early on, for a new mindset among all employees – particularly managers. The new mindset must emphasize customers, service, quality, and looking at the company through the customers' eyes. Introducing such a change in outlook requires a major investment in education for both front line and administration staff.

Fnac, the book, records and hi-fi retail chain, which is based in France but also covers many European countries, left the calm and protected atmosphere of the Co-op, a cooperative distribution group, and went for aggressive development to make profits as well as take on the Virgin Megastore outlets. All managers and employees went through a five-day crash course for mindset change. Some salespeople were reduced to tears during the role-playing exercises because they realized how badly they had treated customers for so many years.

When British Airways launched its crusade for superior service in 1984, all 30,000 employees were invited to a stadium to launch the 'People First' program. When Xerox launched the 'Leadership through Quality' program, starting from the top, waves of managers gave their teams five-day crash courses on the project. And a five-day mindset course was also mandatory for all managers at SKF.

Mindset change includes sessions on the customer's point of view, on quality, on new service standards, and on identifying projects for improvement. Unfortunately changing the mindset often includes changing the teams. British Airways made 64 percent of its middle managers redundant. At SKF a new division was created to service the after-sales market. Its top team was selected not from existing senior managers, but from younger people working in subsidiaries.

Mindset change is best accomplished if led by management, not consultants. As a manager, educating your team results in a stronger belief in what you are preaching. This approach is often facilitated by tools such as role-playing games and other resources that will lead to staff discussing the subject among themselves. In the early 1990s, I was asked to present a conference on customer delight to DSM, a Dutch chemical company. Four years later, they asked me again. Apparently progress had been slow! We decided to design a resource – a game that all managers would learn to play and then take back to their team to use again, with the help of a facilitator. This was designed to spread the word, to get people to express their own way of delighting customers, discuss possible objections, contradictions and so on. The situations were all based on real-life experiences that staff in the business had had.

## Involve

There's a truism that says, 'It is better for customer service to improve 100 details by 1 percent than 1 detail by 100 percent!' Well, is it? What's certain is that, to use your company, the customer must go on an extensive journey

– searching, finding, getting information, choosing, buying, taking delivery, using the product or service, and calling for help. It involves many departments and many contacts with people. When the going gets tough, the contact people are the first to know. They are also the first to know what else your company could bring to customer service. So their involvement in improving present service is crucial. Use feedback from quality teams, service teams, suggestion boxes, team meetings, daily briefings, debriefings after the event, exit interviews with departing colleagues, and good reports from new employees after a month with the company. Here, you ask new employees to tell you what they like and don't like about the company, and what they will use with pride in their own job. Whatever means are used, it is important to open the channels for improving service. In addition, there is a constant need for individuals or project teams to work on delivering new value to the customer in the future. Whether as service process owners and teams, innovation groups, pilot groups, project teams, or creative groups, people from different functions need to be involved in thinking about doing better things. Otherwise the thinking process is too parochial.

A good quality team will produce three to five improvements in current service levels per year. A good service process team will be able to generate and implement one or two significant projects per year.

## Communication

Any change of mindset with respect to customer service is reversible during the initial five years. The temptations are great, and such projects do not always succeed at first. Financial results compete, and there may be a lot of resistance. There will always be people to say, 'I told you it wouldn't work!' In addition, people need to be challenged constantly, and the new mindset needs to be reinforced. Keep asking questions. What have we done for our customers lately? What new service standards should we introduce? What service improvement are we going to emphasize this year? This month? What do new employees need to know about it? What has worked so well that we can spread it around? For each euro spent on implementing the project, another should be spent on communication. For those two reasons – reversibility and reinforcement – you must plan how to communicate the change just as carefully as the content of the change. Here are a few best practices:

- Use literature and tools commonly employed for other purposes to spread the message. If the service campaign uses its own dedicated resources – e.g. a newsletter or a poster – it will be seen as a 'program.' Everybody knows that a program has a beginning and an end. And many people will wait for the 'end.' So it is better to use other media to convey the message. For instance, at a well-known two-star hotel chain, every manager has a book for recording reservations. We redesigned this so that each page carries a reminder of the new service standards. For catering firms, we incorporated tips on events and on briefings with employees in the schedule used by the in-company restaurant. In a hotel chain, we used the daily sheet given to cleaners starting their rounds to remind them of the 10 points to check in a bedroom.

■ Have management communicate the message during their normal meetings. Reinforcements in regular meetings (executive committees, briefings, and forums) are a good way to get the point across again.

■ Design your induction training with care: It is often said that you only get one chance to make a first impression, and it is a long-lasting one. The same applies to employees. The first induction has to convey in a very clear and inspirational manner the emphasis on customer service. It should not simply consist of filling forms and learning the organization chart. At Disney, on the first day of induction, cast members act as 'ghost shoppers' to see how well customers are welcomed and treated. (They are debriefed immediately afterwards.) Some companies even eliminate candidates for an executive position if their knowledge about the company has not included voluntary ghost shopping before the interview took place.

■ Design internal communication campaigns as carefully as you would advertising. You need to break through the clutter of memos, e-mails, and other company noise. Create awareness and a call to action. You need to think about your targets. You need to have an objective: It could be image, action or education. Are you trying to introduce a new service standard, a new service, or a new solution? Don't hesitate to be professional instead of using those ready made posters or that black and white banner which says, 'Let's be passionate for our customers.' I have seen this in a very dull call center where 250 staff members are hemmed in by walls painted in hospital green.

■ Celebrate success. Every advance made on the customer front should be grounds for a celebration. When your idea works, give the credit to your team. When it fails, accept the blame. GrandVision has 400 stores, employing 4,000 people in France. In 1999 the company ordered 10,000 bottles of champagne with the logo GrandVision to celebrate its retail successes.

- Involve customers in sharing satisfaction issues. Once a year, companies like Texas Instruments, Adecco or Dow invite their customers to discuss results of satisfaction surveys, or issues related to their partnerships, or both. A few customers are invited to give their views and discuss them with senior management.

- Post the results of satisfaction surveys and compliments everywhere: Don't keep them hidden in your market research department. Don't put them as lists of statistics. People should be able to read them at a glance. This means simple graphs and appealing visuals.

## Quick wins

When bearings company SKF embarked on a targeted service strategy for the after sales market – replacing ball bearings in machines in industry and garages – one of the first things it did was to set up five new service standards. These included such basic things as answering the phone within three rings, or answering a request from another department within half a day. Were those five objectives the key to the success of the service strategy? Certainly not. Answering the phone quickly is not at the core of customer needs and expectations in the bearings business. However, it gave a signal, and it was a quick win. Quick wins are necessary to create momentum in what could be a very long journey to success. As I have already said, in large companies five years of motivation is necessary to ensure the organization will not revert to old behavior. But most large companies agree that it will take about 10 years for the new strategy to have its full impact. And long lead times are inevitable in some areas. As we have seen, service encounters are of three types, one being the transaction (Chapter 3). Transactions have to do with systems which, in turn, are bound up with information technology (IT), an area where projects often take forever (or at least three years). In the meantime, managers need to be able to demonstrate some progress. Here are four pointers towards a quick win.

- The customer satisfaction program can be a module of the IT program. That is how Hewlett-Packard managed it, when the company decided to create key accounts to sell its PCs and peripherals across Europe. The first module was an online system that enabled key account managers to know the availability of merchandise when facing customers.

- It can happen as a pilot site or country or function. That is how Midas convinced its franchisees the program was worth investing in.

- It can be a department. The customer service department, where all complaints from customers are received, is often a good place to start.

It's also where problems voiced by the customer all end up. I have even recommended that any senior executive who is going to be in charge of a unit should spend six months to a year there as part of his or her 'training.' After such an experience, a manager will appreciate the implications of any decision that could affect service negatively.

▥ It can focus on a particular customer group. At Microsoft, after the first survey was completed, operations in all countries were asked to concentrate on the dissatisfied customers. The focus could be key accounts, new accounts, or the Z-customer. The Z-customer is one who has gone from pillar to post, from A to B, to C right down to Z in accumulated dissatisfaction, and is ready to quit. In certain sectors where the costs of switching suppliers are high, customers tend to stick around longer, until eventually the pain is too great. Such losses can easily be predicted by studying the pattern of dissatisfaction among lost customers. Thus one may rescue these relationships before it is too late.

## Creating customer-centered structures and processes

Most classical organization structures are centered on 'product' (or service), geography or function. Two issues arise when a service strategy is defined:

▥ Can the same people serve all customers, or should your company have dedicated coverage for each service segment?

▥ In each function, do you have a way of treating different customer requirements differently?

When SKF changed direction to serve the after sales market, it decided it needed a different structure. The existing company served OEMs mainly, and was organized by function and factory. It was selling on the basis of volume/price/just-in-time. But in the after-sales market, industrial customers needed a preventive maintenance package that included products other than bearings (lubricants for example) and services such as consulting. It would have been very difficult for volume-oriented factories to turn themselves into advisors and sell these new products. A new structure, reflecting the company's customers, had to be put in place.

This is also what Microsoft has done by restructuring its management team, following the decision to focus on customer satisfaction. Microsoft was previously organized by product groups (Windows, Office, and Online). This is to be replaced by four customer divisions: consumer, knowledge workers, IT professionals, and developers. Underlying this is the understanding that these four customer segments have very different needs.

- Consumers seek user-friendly programs and are averse to frequent updates.

- Knowledge workers want sophisticated functions, without glitches.

- IT professionals demand products that can be distributed quickly throughout an organization with minimal need for support.

- Developers want early access, involvement in updates, new features, and corrections.

Again, it would have been difficult for factories to put into effect a package of measures catering for all these needs. In many cases, then, it is necessary to split the organization to ensure that different segments are served, and that the new customer value is implemented, instead of merely forcing changes upon the current structure. In addition, within each function – whether IT or marketing – there is a need to align the structure according to customer segment. Let's see how this would work in the marketing department of a company. The classical structure of such departments is illustrated in Figure 6.2. A more customer focused strategy could look like that in Figure 6.3. This also means all functions and departments need to be linked by a simple answer to a simple question: How does my department contribute to customer service?

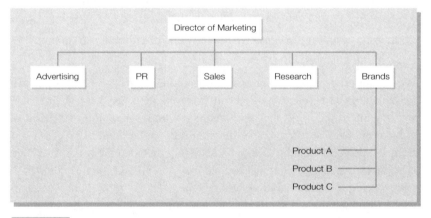

**Figure 6.2**    Traditional structure of a marketing department

Organizing for the customer, then, is at the strategic business unit level whether at the division/country/customer segment (like SKF or Microsoft) or department level (as in Figure 6.3).

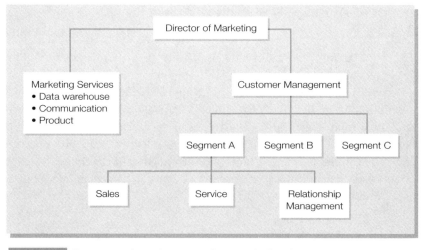

**Figure 6.3**   Customer-oriented structure for a marketing department

## Same roof or different roofs for different customer segments?

Not only can a structure be more customer-centered, but, as the above example of SKF shows, maybe it should not even be under the same roof (i.e. be under the same general manager's responsibility or even in the same physical location), to have a chance to develop and thrive. A structure by customer segments or geography is not always the answer. For instance, cellphone service operators always distinguish business-to-business from business-to-consumer businesses. Different customers, different value propositions, different distributors, different sales force.

However, suppose that the cellphone service provider now wants to create a new service in which it would cut all the 'frills' in order to provide a 'no frills' mobile service, *à la* easyJet. Should it stay within the same organization or move out of it? That is, should marketing, distribution, and the call center report to the same bosses as the current business, or should a separate company be created? It may result in duplication of resources, but it provides more chance to focus on what is key to succeed in the new business. Creating an entirely separate company – a different roof – may be necessary to stay completely customer centered.

## Key account managers should become key customer managers!

The word 'account' does not lend itself to being customer oriented. Key customer manager, key customer relationship manager, or even manager for key customer relationships would probably fit better, as long as the job description is in line with the title. When key account managers are appointed in an organization, two opposing forces can often be observed. On the one hand, the key account manager's role is to make sure that the company's interests are well protected, defended, and developed. On the other hand, the customer's interests must be best defended and developed, as shown in Figure 6.4.

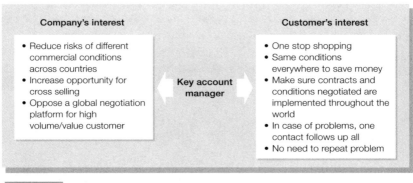

**Figure 6.4**    Objectives for the key account manager

We could argue that these two forces are not necessarily contradictory, and sum up the role of the key customer manager under one job description:

- Fully understand the needs of the key customer, and disseminate this knowledge throughout the organization.

- Get the different parts of the organization to propose the best value(s) for those needs, and agree on an overall contract and conditions.

- Get the organization to deliver seamlessly on the value proposition anywhere, any time.

- In case of problems, queries and questions, act as a go-between to reduce animosity and coordinate problem-solving.

- Be the voice of the key customer within the organization to help improve and innovate.

- Success of key customer is measured in:
  - sales/growth in sales for that key customer;
  - key customer satisfaction;

- speed of complaint handling and problem solving;
- length of relationship of customer;
- reduction of problems thanks to inputs from key customers;
- reduction in costs to key customer for handling transactions with the supplier.

Are your key account managers measured on these criteria?

## Correcting natural tendencies of organizational structures to forget customers

There is no perfect organization structure. Each architecture has its advantages and drawbacks.

■ Organizing by function favors efficiency and cost reduction.

■ Organizing by geography favors closeness to the markets.

■ Organizing by segment favors responsiveness to customer needs.

■ Organizing by business unit favors entrepreneurship and marketing.

It is not always feasible to change a structure to be closer to the customer, as was described in the last section. However, some mechanisms (processes or organizational) can help keep the customer at the center of a company's thoughts. They can complement the development of a customer culture and customer-centric managerial behavior. Those mechanisms include the use of *ad hoc* committees, the appointment of coordinators for particular customers or customer needs, hybrid organization structure, use of transfer prices to reinforce customer orientation, job rotation among key players, and the use of key performance indicators aimed at spotting customer issues. And finally, there is the identification and ownership of customers' processes.

■ *Ad hoc* committees composed of both decision makers and field people close to customers can help – especially in functional structures – to identify customer service issues, find solutions, and follow up on execution. Such committees can tackle issues such as customer complaints, new product development, logistics, and the demand chain. At Disney Parks the creative marketing committee meets once a month. The creative team responsible for shows teams up with the marketing team to identify what they have in mind and whether it will attract more guests, and then mutually adjust. It is chaired by the CEO.

Committees work best when decisions are made at the end of each meeting.

■ Coordinators can be appointed to coordinate areas missed in the existing structure. For instance, when marketing is organized by function (pricing, communication, sales, etc.), a segment manager can try to combine the efforts of the sales, market research, and after sales service departments for the benefit of a particular segment.

■ Hybrid structures provide a way to take into account both the use of common shared resources and expertise for maximum effectiveness and customer orientation. Like any complex structure, it is rather difficult to manage without a common culture and objectives that lead to good cooperation. A geographical structure could still benefit from centralized production and logistics, provided the production people recognize that the geography is their internal customer. A strategic business unit could use central services (IT and HR), provided it experiences the same level of service as if it were buying from the outside!

■ Transfer prices: Books can be written on the subject! Each time a transfer price is decided, it creates certain behaviors that go for or against the customers. To minimize the negative impact on customers, the first step is to define what behavior is necessary to be successful in the marketplace with customers; then set up a tentative transfer price; then test it on the company decision makers to see how they are likely to behave, and modify accordingly.

Recently, I was asked to discuss customer orientation with one of the world's leading marine coatings companies. They had noted that there has been a shift from many small shipyards to a few large ones, and from a large number of ship owners or operators to very few (at least in certain parts of the world). In the past the shipyards were organized by geography to be close to the customer. The new ones require cooperation between local sale and service offices in order to stay customer-focused and driven. A ship owner in Greece could, for instance, sign a product/service contract with the Greek office. However, the ships could be inspected and maintained by other offices around the world. What transfer price and contribution should be given to the other offices to make them understand that the Greek customer is a priority? If too little attention is paid, large international customers may be less well served than a local customer. If too much attention is paid, the initiator of the lead might not see much on their own profit and loss, even though he has generated the business. Of course, transfer prices might not be the long-term solution if trends towards globalization of customers become even bigger (a global key customer account could do better), but in the meantime, the wrong behavior could adversely affect performance.

Transfer prices are necessary for shared resources and services (production, IT, etc.) serving customers across geographical or product boundaries, and expected behavior of the managers should be the driving force. As an alternative, one way to avoid transfer prices is to pool performance when people need to work together into a combined P&L for the part of their activity they do together.

■ Job rotation provides a good way to see someone else's viewpoint within the organization. It can consist of short-term appointments (take my seat for a day or a week and I will take yours) – this works well between staff positions and line positions. Or it can be longer term. For instance, Nestlé uses job rotation between headquarters and the field. In their career, between two line management appointments in a particular business in a particular geographical area, people will spend two to four years at the headquarters in Vevey to get a global perspective.

■ Heavy customer presence in the Key Performance Indicators (KPI) can be used to drive the business. One way to keep track of customers in an organizational structure (especially those which by essence are not customer focused and organized by function, by factory or by zone) is to make sure that, in the design and implementation of KPIs, customer issues are measured in such way that they are felt to be the responsibility of all. Take a typical functional structure with R&D, marketing and sales, production, logistics, and after sales service. Who is responsible for customer satisfaction? Marketing and sales because they have identified the needs? Logistics and production because they have delivered? R&D because they have invented the right product? After sales service because they have fixed problems the other departments have created? In fact, all! Measurements must be designed in such a way that all departments know how they contribute to overall customer satisfaction as well as provide a clear assessment of the relative impact of each function on overall satisfaction, loyalty, and thus growth and profits. It could look like the chart shown in Figure 6.5.

■ Customer activities and customer process ownership: The best engineered organization structures can lose track of customers even if they use the above mechanisms such as transfer price and job rotation. The 'business' part and short-term pressure on P&L tend to diminish closeness to customers. In hybrid organizations such as the matrix organization, it is sometimes even worse. Even managers get lost in them – let alone customers' interests!

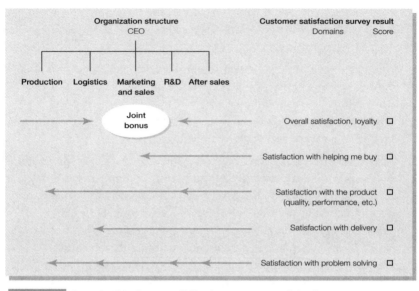

**Figure 6.5**    Organizational responsibility for customer satisfaction

One way to avoid losing track of customers is to focus on processes rather than structure – i.e., describe customer activities and assign responsibility for the underlying processes that will make the activity fruitful for the customer.

Let's take a simple set of tasks of a typical customer who buys and uses industrial goods (Figure 6.6). There are several underlying company processes that need to be in place to satisfy customers, and these processes need to have more than one function. For instance, for a proposal to be a good one from the customer's viewpoint, R&D, products, marketing and sales, and maybe logistics are involved. By appointing a 'proposal' process owner responsible for getting the organizational act together, maybe the hit rate (i.e. how many proposals are transferred into a sale) can increase!

Many companies have divided their processes into several groups and appointed process owners, but the perspective is often internal. Rather than being customer value oriented, it is focused on cost cutting. It is a new 'reengineering' that is proposed here to get the process owner to look at the most effective horizontal way of fulfilling the customer's concerns.

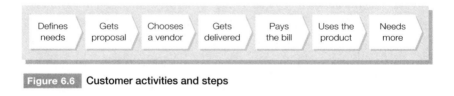

**Figure 6.6**    Customer activities and steps

## Replacing business processes by customer processes

Imagine that you are a retailer selling eyeglasses in one hour. Imagine that you want to take a new look at your processes, as you are not satisfied with their effectiveness. In order to do so, you would like to identify each process so that you can describe them as they are today, then ask yourself how to achieve the same output but more effectively (cheaper, faster, etc.). Classical business reengineering would probably lead you to identify the key main processes, as shown in Figure 6.7. You could add to it some support processes such as finance and control, HR, etc. Working on each of those processes would make it simpler to reduce costs and to speed up. It would make it more difficult, however, to be customer centric.

**Figure 6.7**   Business processes in optical retailing

Now, suppose that you change focus toward the customer, and ask yourself what processes need to work well for the customer to be happy. You might probably come up with the following customer centric ideas.

▓ One hour delivery, which in turn requires the capability to assemble frame and lenses in one hour or less.

▓ The fit process: the ability to propose glasses and frame which fit the customer needs, so that he or she is happy with the glasses chosen.

▓ The replacement process in case the customer loses or breaks his glasses.

▓ The personalization process: the ability to propose something unique (custom made) or corresponding to past tastes and behavior.

▓ The value process: offering products and services at a price that makes people want to buy from us.

Personalization, replacement, and being able to fit in one hour are all customer benefits. They cut across several 'business processes.' A solution brought to improve those customer processes will have repercussions in purchasing, marketing, and retailing.

It is also possible to use the customer activity cycle over time as a useful guide to customer processes. As an example, let's look at the steps the customer goes through to buy and use a floor carpet. There are four key steps, as shown in Figure 6.8.

| Pre-purchase | Purchase | Delivery | Usage |
|---|---|---|---|
| • Looking for alternative floor covering<br>• Obtaining quotes | • Choosing a merchant<br>• Choosing the carpet that fits house and furniture | • Getting delivery date<br>• Getting rid of the old carpet<br>• Preparing floor installation | • Cleaning<br>• Removing stains<br>• Adapting new furniture to carpet<br>• Adding carpeting |

**Figure 6.8**   **The four key steps**                    *Source: Dupont case, © 1993 IMD*

These are processes that a carpet retailer can improve in order to gain customers and keep them, provided he can see beyond just the purchase process. And, in fact, this was the approach chosen by Dupont to improve its insight on how to promote floor carpeting for which it provided fibers. This approach shifts the emphasis of process engineering dramatically.

Recently, I was presented the business-to-business activities for a cellphone operator in Sweden, as illustrated in Figure 6.9. This is inward looking and mostly confined to the marketing department. From a customer viewpoint, the activities might look like those illustrated in Figure 6.10. Having someone responsible for each customer activity will force the marketing department, the call center, and the international network to work together for better customer value!

| • Shipping cellphones | • Calling after 1 month to see if properly used | • Calling after 6 months to propose additional services | • Sending a newsletter every 2 months for update | • Calling after 18 months to propose upgrade |
|---|---|---|---|---|

**Figure 6.9**   **Marketing activities for a cellphone operator**

| • He receives his phone and needs to transfer existing data into it | • He learns how to use it | • He has problems | • He receives the first bill |
|---|---|---|---|
| • He wants to change | • He leaves the company | • He is transferred abroad | |

**Figure 6.10**   **Customer activities for a cellphone user**

## A customer-centric process analysis and responsibility setting needs the following steps

■ Start by identifying the key customer benefits that you plan to offer, as the optical retail chain explored.

■ Alternatively identify the key steps the customer goes through to buy and use the service, as was shown in the carpet and cellphone examples.

■ Appoint a 'process owner' and a team to describe each customer benefit or each customer activity and the corresponding internal current processes (and sub-processes), and see where they could be improved. Team members will come from the different 'classical' departments or functions existing in the firm.

■ Select criteria for 'process' improvements:
  - add value to the customer (more benefits, or better solution to customer activities)
  - improve delivery of customer value (i.e. fewer defects);
  - reduce the costs.

■ Implement in each function with the process owner coordinating.

## Put your money where your mouth is

As long as customer satisfaction, or customer service quality, or whatever you want to call it is excluded from the normal planning/budgeting/resource allocation cycle, it will remain a 'program.' It will wither and die, usually with the departure of the senior executive who started it or the consultant responsible for its introduction.

Customer satisfaction needs to be an integral part of the normal planning, decision-making, and budgeting process. This implies that:

■ Specific objectives must be set.

■ Action plans must be spelled out.

■ Responsibilities must be assigned to executives, and the plan defined.

■ Obstacles to measuring progress have to be identified (dates, intermediate goals).

■ Budgets must be allocated.

Since customer satisfaction affects most of the organization, project leadership teams must be nominated to monitor progress and make things happen. Generally speaking, any customer satisfaction/service idea that is not included in the plan will not happen over time. When Société Générale decided to embark on a quality program for its corporate finance division, the management nominated someone to follow the process in each region of the world, and in each division. That person was responsible for eliciting one project from line management and working with them to make it happen during the planning period.

When Microsoft launched its customer satisfaction program, within three months the managers in each country were working on between 50 and 100 ideas for improvement. Priorities were set up for each country and budgets allocated. It is hoped that if customers are satisfied, word-of-mouth recommendation will follow, which will lead to more customers, which will lead to more sales.

It's less easy to say that we will cut advertising and use all the money saved to increase customer satisfaction. What is true for costs is also true for investments: for example in IT. IT people often want to spend too much, and imply that the whole organization will collapse if the systems, hardware, and software are not modified to the point that they represent up to 4 percent on sales! Suppose you ask the department to split all their investments into at least three of the four categories shown in Figure 6.11.

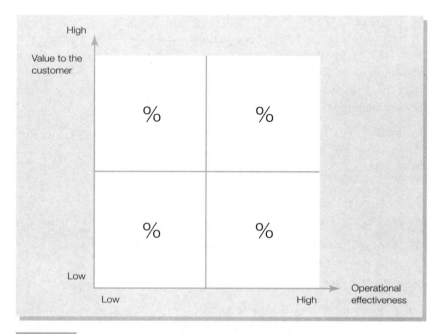

**Figure 6.11**    IT investments and their value to customers

■ How much should be spent in each category?

■ How much do we currently spend in each (and how much has been spent in the past)? What changes must be made to spend enough for clients and less for ourselves?

The same goes for other investments: Should we redecorate our offices or the reception desk? Install more workstations to answer more calls at peak hours, or buy new accounting software? By tracing investments, one can easily tell whether a company is really committed to serving customers. There are emergencies, and infrastructures need to be upgraded, but if action goes where the money flows, the changes should be visible.

# Measure and follow up

## Process of measuring the right things

Chapter 4 was devoted to this topic, so I shall not go over the same ground, but some thought should be given to the process of measuring, as well as its content. You always need to measure before you start anything. This will provide a benchmark of where you stand with your customers. Measurement helps set targets. Measurement should be carried out at the level where people can identify their own problem and feel the challenge to do better. Otherwise staff might say, 'It's not for my department (or site/region/product line/country) but a problem for somewhere else.' Measurements should include need analysis, the satisfaction of occasional customers, and employee satisfaction. Customer satisfaction and employee satisfaction work in parallel. Satisfied employees lead to satisfied customers. Good internal service contributes to good external service.

Intervals between measurements should be dictated by the time that it takes to implement change. If measurements are too frequent, people become discouraged because they see no progress. But if measurements are too few and far between, they will not show cause and effect clearly enough, and will fail to spur progress. As noted in Chapter 4, your company should not confine itself to measuring whether it is doing things right (current operations), but should also ask whether it is doing the right things (strategic analysis). The results of measurements should be widely known, accessible, visualized, discussed, and acted upon. Too often I have seen vast, indigestible measurement reports filed away in managers' offices. They need to reach all front line employees.

Finally, avoid those surveys that exploit satisfaction as a pretext for finding out more about the customer for marketing purposes. In such surveys, more than half of the questions may be devoted to marketing rather than the customer's perception of the company. If you need to carry out market research, that is a separate issue. If you mix both, you risk irritating your customers and getting a low response. A good system should give you a response of 60 to 90 percent for business-to-business and 40 to 90 percent for consumers.

## Process of linking rewards to service excellence

In 1994 Disneyland Paris turned itself around from a debt-ridden, loss-making company to a profitable venture by creating a new structure. Twelve hierarchical levels were reduced to three: directors, small world managers, and cast members. In effect, it divided its overall structure – encompassing 12,000 cast members – into 250 small worlds, with each manager heading 40 to 50 cast members. For each small world, performance and bonuses were assessed on three, equally weighted factors: customer satisfaction, cast member satisfaction, and economic result (cost, revenue, or profit).

When Xerox embarked on its program of change, it introduced a team bonus at district level: The sales manager, delivery manager, and after-sales manager jointly got their bonuses, based on customer satisfaction. Our behavior is often linked to the rewards we receive, in the form of promotions, incentives, recognition and so on. I have never seen bank branch managers getting the senior jobs. Since these are the people in contact with customers, this speaks volumes about the importance of customers in banks' strategies.

There is no place for conflicting signals. A company proclaiming that customer service strategy is all, while rewarding people for doing something else, is not paying out on its promise. Service-linked rewards must be implemented at all levels, including at senior executive level. Show me what proportion of the top team bonus is based on customer satisfaction and I will tell you whether you really mean what you say about customer service in those annual speeches!

## Follow-up

It is natural to follow up any project to see it through to completion. Xerox's program singled out initiatives linked to customer satisfaction for special attention.

- Project teams followed up implementation of initiatives.
- The executive committee devoted one out of every three regular meeting exclusively to the topic.

■ Special assignments were given to allow staff to follow up complaints and respond promptly (a quick win).

When GrandOptical launched its seven-point guarantee of total customer satisfaction (see Chapter 4), it appointed a manager to follow up on each of the seven points. For instance, one point guaranteed: 'We will make your glasses in one hour or deliver them free anywhere you want.' Here, follow-up meant knowing how many times free deliveries were needed, on what products, in which stores, on what day, and at what cost for which type of customer. The objective was not to minimize delivery cost but to improve the one-hour score!

Many customer satisfaction initiatives get buried, lost, or forgotten because they are not followed up at the highest level. Questions must be asked continually. What is the status? How do you make progress? What has been done? What are the priorities for next year? What were the results like? What do you expect? Does the company have an exchange of best practices or does it re-invent the wheel in different departments? What indicators do we have for follow-up?

Only with such a systematic approach will a strategy get implemented. And it is at this stage that projects fail most often.

# CRM investments: beware

Many companies invest hefty sums into CRM as if it were the holy grail of management processes that will resolve every customer related issue once and for all. Well, it might be useful to deflate the ever-expanding balloon of CRM a little.

In 2002, *McKinsey Quarterly* published an article entitled 'How to rescue CRM.' It proposed an approach intended to save the investments that companies have poured into CRM over the years. In the US, this is estimated to be about $4 billion per year just in software. Add to that figure some $12–20 billion for implementation, integration, and training. To look at it another way, for a large company that's €100 million and three years' work for a success rate of between 25 and 40 percent, according to research carried out by Gartner in 2002.

This mirage is of worrying proportions. A study by International Data Corporation in 2002 of decision makers revealed that 68 percent of respondents said they expected an increase in revenue of 10 percent or less from their CRM efforts. Another study of decision makers by International Data

Corporation indicated that just 35 percent felt their expectations had been met by CRM. And a 2002 Gartner satisfaction study from vendor ratings speaks for itself. Ten percent of vendors are excellent and only 33 percent manage 'good.' So what is the issue, and how do you minimize the risk of failure?

Two issues stand out: lack of preparation, and lack of commitment.

1  *Lack of preparation*: To invest in CRM software cannot be the miracle that will transform a whole company from product to service, from inward looking to customer focused. CRM is just a tool that helps improve whatever we are already doing.

   Some questions to assess your level of preparedness:
   – Are we already customer focused?
   – Do we already do whatever we can to know our customers, listen to them, react to their problems, and proactively propose solutions to their individual needs?
   – Do we use our current contacts (truck drivers, support staff, accounting, repair man, call center, etc.) to their fullest advantage to give more information, propose new solutions, get more inputs, solve problems fast and maintain relationships?
   – Do we already use all our knowledge about our customers, their pattern of consumption, their behavior, and their stated problems to personalize our response, to cater to their individual needs, to present our apologies, and to make up for our failures?
   – Do we act to propose better support, or do we only react to circumstances?
   – Do we already do the utmost – and to their satisfaction – for our customers who have had problems with us or have complained? This is an acid test of preparedness. If we are not able to react positively to customers who do not need a database or mining or warehousing because they have identified themselves as needing care, then how could we handle the increased numbers of customers that a CRM system will churn out?
   – Is every customer who is known in one department or function also known in other departments?

2  *Commitment* is the second hurdle to CRM. Commitment is about the willingness to put resources where our analysis tells us they should be put. Suppose the system helps us detect four segments with four different sets of needs. Are we prepared to act? Are we prepared to put our money where our mouth is? Are we able to change our ways of

conducting business to get closer to customer relationships? Take the following example of heavy users of cellphones in France. They are usually busy people needing their phone all day long. So a double or even a triple SIM card is necessary to make it convenient for the customer to call (and for the phone companies to get more billings!). However, having more than one SIM card means you need to be able to put all calls from all SIM cards on the same bill. This is not done in France! No resources have so far been put into systems to provide two or more SIM cards to those heavy users. However, all cellphone providers have bought a CRM system! What for?

Grupo Financiero Bital is a leading financial services provider in Mexico. Gartner Group research has ranked them as the best CRM implementer in 2002. Bital has six million customers, 1,350 branches and 15,400 employees, with a market share of around 15 percent. It recognized that greater customer intimacy was key to developing a competitive advantage. What did it do?

■ Segment its market into three target customer types.

■ Adapt the value proposition/pricing to each.

■ Organize for collaboration among departments.

■ Redesign its management processes to attract, satisfy, retain, and grow its customers.

■ Use new technology to receive all of the data from all transactional systems over three years.

■ Set up metrics for performance.

The results were quite impressive: 20 to 30 percent response to new product offerings; 12 percent new credit accounts; retention rate increased from 77 to 90 percent; and a 20 percent increase in customer loyalty. (Source: Gartner, research R 18-5681 December 2002.)

## Summary

In this chapter, we have looked at the management processes required for moving an organization towards customers and customer orientation, namely:

■ Focused objectives that lead to results, once the stakes are known.

■ A shift in organization structure and customer process ownership.

■ A change management process to create a mindset. Get quick wins, involve people and redesign incentives that fit the purpose, to gain everyone's commitment.

- A new revised planning and resource allocation process that demonstrates our commitment and follow-up.

This is a systematic effort that can either be done on a pilot basis if too much resistance is met, or be rolled out company wide. But it cannot be half done!

# Don'ts

1 Don't delegate quality to a director of quality. It is a top management call requiring top management attention.

2 Don't wait until you have designed all the tools to get initiatives started in the field. Start with pilot projects, customer segments and so on.

3 Don't underestimate the number of management changes necessary to accompany your strategy: structure, processes, measurement, follow-up.

4 Don't be economical with incentives, follow-ups, and mindset changes. Put your money where your mouth is.

5 Don't treat it as a program, but as a process – a journey.

6 Don't give up – it takes time.

7 Don't think it is natural. Dinosaurs need to be shaken up.

8 Don't embark on a full program if everything is okay. You won't find followers. Get quick wins first.

9 And *do* start with a pilot.

# The 10 structure and processes questions

1 Do you know what you can gain by providing better service to customers?

2 Is your organization oriented towards the customer?

3 Have you developed objectives for customer satisfaction improvement?

4 Is there a link between service/satisfaction and rewards?

5 How involved are your people in improving customer service?

6 Is your company mindset oriented toward the customer?

7 Do you have regular internal communications about customers?

8 Does your next three year plan specifically include projects for improving customer service?

9 Do you know what projects are carried out to deal specifically with service?

10 What were your quick wins in the last six months? And what will they be in the next six months?

# 7

# Company culture and customer relationships

The quality of service delivered by your company depends, at least partly, on how your staff interact with customers. So from this standpoint alone, it is natural to look in some depth at how people are managed. Does your company's people management meet particular service requirements and affect service performance? Chapter 2 describe the three types of encounter that can happen between customers and your company:

- Physical (documentation, merchandise).

- Transaction (delivery, speed).

- Interaction (dealings with company employees).

The impact of good people management can be tremendous; its influence extends beyond interaction encounters to the other types.

Motivated employees will make transaction encounters smooth and cost effective. There is, in fact, a strong link between motivation and productivity in the service area. Physical encounters are on the front line, as are the staff who orchestrate them, taking care of delivery trucks, presenting merchandise in an appealing way, keeping the place clean, and so on. In addition, employee motivation through involvement and empowerment favors not only a speedy resolution of customers' problems but also results in quality improvements, making both transactions and physical encounters smoother and more appealing.

Many books have been written on this topic, yet it is amazing to see how few companies really invest in motivating their people to give good customer service. In this chapter I will not reiterate the positive measures a company should undertake to put employees at the center of its service strategy. Instead, this chapter presents three dimensions of people management, developed while observing and working in different service industries:

- Adapting to different requirements of the service business.
- The manager's new role: coach.
- Creating a proper culture to foster customer orientation.

# Different service requirements

There is a tendency to admire companies that deliver excellent service through their staff. Thus companies such as Disney, McDonald's, Superquinn or First Direct are constantly benchmarked to inspire people management practices in other organizations. Other firms analyze in detail how they recruit, train, develop, motivate, and reward, in an attempt to find new ways of managing their own service people. Sometimes this is only to find out that the imported techniques do not always work. Then management is quick to present arguments suggesting industry differences ('It is good for the entertainment industry, but not for the financial service industry'). Even worse, failure is explained away as a result of cultural differences ('It's too American') or competencies ('It might be true for unskilled people, but does not apply to bankers') or size ('We cannot do that in a big company'). Experience with more than 100 European and US service companies leads me to believe that the key driver of optimal service people management is not industrial sector, nor education, nor the culture of the country in which the company is located. It is in the nature of the service provided, based on two dimensions:

1  Duration (and frequency) of contact.

2  Intensity of interaction.

This is depicted schematically in Figure 7.1.

## Duration of contact

Some services require a long duration of contact between the service provider's staff and the customer, while others only require a brief – even if frequent – contact. For instance, the average customer will have 30 seconds' contact with a steward or stewardess on a transatlantic flight in chunks of 5–10 seconds. During a hotel stay, an average visitor might have five minutes of contact with staff, spread out over a few days and among several employees. Contact with the staff of a software solution provider, on the other hand, could go on for hours. The longer the duration, and the greater the frequency of contact, the more you need to ensure a consistent level of

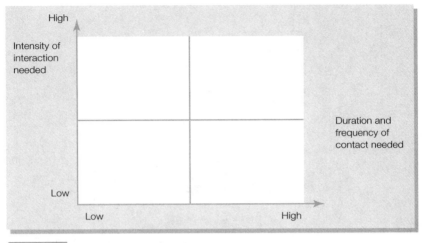

**Figure 7.1**    Two dimensions of service

quality in the various encounters, whether the customer is met by a single employee repeatedly or by different people at different times. If customers are made welcome at the reception desk in a hotel, they need to feel the same sort of welcome in the restaurant, and get a consistent, welcoming attitude by cleaners and other staff, to leave with a good overall impression. If an assistant is pleasant the first time he or she meets a customer, that attitude should be maintained for subsequent meetings, even if each encounter lasts no longer than five seconds. Any service that requires either an extended contact with a particular person or a series of short but frequent dealings with different staff members (as in a health farm, retail store, restaurant, or museum) comes under the heading 'long duration of contact.'

## Intensity of interaction

In many services, although contact between staff and customers is prolonged, the interaction is not very intensive. It may require no more than a few words, some simple advice, and information based on a transaction. Consider a restaurant. The main interaction supplied by a host or hostess could be as simple as a few stock phrases:

- 'How many are you?'
- 'A table for five?'
- 'Please follow me.'
- 'Enjoy your dinner.'

However, in other services the interaction is much more intense. Examples that spring to mind are education, psychotherapy, technical support,

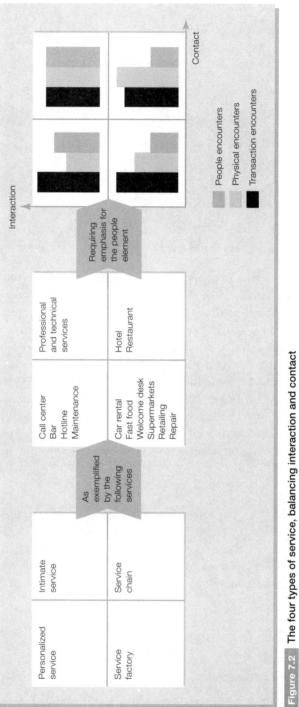

**Figure 7.2**  The four types of service, balancing interaction and contact

hotlines, fire, accidents, and technical or advisory selling. Here staff must probe customers, analyze their needs, identify problems, provide solutions, answer objections, listen to them, and so on. Any service that involves intensive interaction – either as a one off or repeatedly over time – will require individuals who can stand on their feet, react quickly and autonomously without having to ask a boss, and face different situations all the time. Unless these individuals can function completely alone (either because of personal qualities or educational qualifications) the company will be in trouble. On the other hand, low-intensity situations demand only relatively standardized, non-innovative responses from staff.

Taking into account these two dimensions of interaction – intensity and duration – one can perceive four distinct types of service, each needing a different approach to human resources management. Each type also needs a different type of staff. However, I have not emphasized the people element of service at the expense of the other two contributors to service: systems transactions and physical surroundings. Figure 7.2 shows the four service types as a series of charts. Figure 7.3 identifies the resulting key profile requirement for each type of service.

In turn, these charts specify the human resources competencies necessary to deliver good interaction, as shown in Table 7.1.

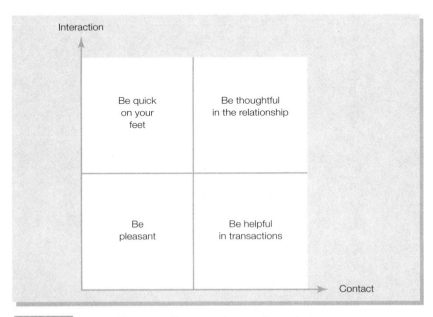

**Figure 7.3**  Staff profiles according to service requirement

**Table 7.1    Human resources requirements and service requirements**

|  | Service factory:<br>Be pleasant | Service chain:<br>Be helpful | Service personalization:<br>Be quick on your feet | Service intimacy:<br>Be thoughtful |
|---|---|---|---|---|
| Recruitment | Pleasant, honest, young, adaptable, first job, low pay | Pleasant, honest, young with some professional technical skills. Long induction | Professionals already trained on technical skills before joining | Professionals with a strong personality |
| Training | Product/ Service/ Company Quick training on basics for front line. Heavy competencies training for supervisors of managers | Training of front line on company culture, service quality and professional training. Training of managers as coaches | On objectives. With mentors. Frequent updates or new techniques | Mentoring. Exchanges of best practices. Company culture. Professional competencies improvement |
| Development | Don't let people stay – manage turnover through good supervision | Internal promotion is key to reinforce the quality of service chain | Trips. Site changes | Internal promotion |

| | | | |
|---|---|---|---|
| Motivation | Celebrate to keep the spirit up. Create a campus-like ambience | Treat employees as customers. Career opportunities | Manage ups and downs of each individual through praise and affirmation like fostering of 'artists'. Initiatives through unlimited empowerment, education | Initiative. 'Bravos' from customers. Made to feel like a family. Frequent rotation of job to avoid boredom and keep energy level high. New challenges. Continuous education |
| Organizational support | Procedures manual. Close supervision Smooth administrative matters. Fast induction | Help desk or escalation for difficult questions. Good staff planning | Sound, flawless systems put in place | All non-customer-oriented problems taken care of by administration and service departments |
| Involvement | Quality circles | Cross functional quality teams | Project teams | Cross functional project teams |
| Empowerment for recovery of dissatisfied customer | Limited to small initiatives in case of complaints (with escalation) | Works within a pre-defined list of actions/initiatives (with escalation) | Full initiatives within the job | Full empowerment even for someone else's job |

# Four ways to lead people

This section looks at how four leading companies in different fields and with different service strategies manage staff who come into contact with customers.

## The service factory strategy: United Parcel Service

UPS is a mail delivery service similar to Federal Express. This is a business in which interaction is low and duration is short (except when there is a problem, and even then it varies from problem to problem). The human resource levers employed to deliver UPS's services are very specific to its strategy. UPS invests time in standardizing know-how and training people to follow standard procedures. Using time-and-motion studies, more than 3,000 engineers design ways of performing tasks. Drivers, for example, are told how to carry packages and even how to fold money (face up). The level of job-enrichment is low and supervision is high. Individual involvement and commitment is also low. Performance is measured individually against standards that have been set for each task. As compensation, people receive substantial material rewards: The company pays the highest wages in the industry, and offers profit-sharing and stock ownership. In addition, UPS offers long-term prospects for advancement. Entry-level employees are given opportunities to move up the ladder and make a career in the company. Almost all promotions are from within.

## The service chain: Disney

In Disney parks, the service chain is important: The total experience is what will make the customer happy. This total experience starts at the hotel, continues in the park, and finishes perhaps at Disney village, the off-park evening entertainment venue. Usually the company seeks cast members with a positive attitude toward service, and trains them locally (two days' induction and from one to four weeks of professional training). In addition, in areas such as cooking, gardening, and maintenance many employees must have technical qualifications. Training is an integral part of cast members' development, enabling them to change jobs or move to a higher level in the same job (teamleader, for instance). Level of skills will be associated with higher pay. All world managers, each leading a team of around 50 cast members, get an intensive 12-day training course on leadership, service quality, and business. Internal promotion is the preferred mode of development. Cast members create many occasions for celebration, including shows and musical events. The best are recognized as 'cast members of the month' or of the year. After one, five, and ten years with the company they receive a medal and, again, are given a celebration.

## Personalized service: Microsoft

At Microsoft customer support service, interaction is important, but its duration is expected to be brief. In fact, technical support involves many questions from both sides and advice being dispensed to the customers in order to solve their specific software or computer-related problems. Microsoft customer support engineers are recruited for qualities such as empathy, an aptitude for teaching and solving other people's problems: analytical problem-solving and communication skills.

Training is essentially on technique and communication. It consists of three to four weeks on MS-DOS and Windows, plus general training on communication skills with a module on how to handle customers. Then customer support engineers learn on the job. They go on to specialize, and receive an additional two-week course on a particular application. During this specialization period, before manning the phones they listen in on phone calls, work with mentors (one mentor for every eight technicians), and answer letters from customers. After specialization, there is a continuous training of about 20 hours per employee per year.

Motivation is based on entrepreneurial incentives (Microsoft offers the opportunity to make money from buying shares), a career path in the company, and association with the Microsoft reputation, which opens doors to other companies. Career prospects are based on progress up a ladder, which is unusual in the high-tech business. A typical career path is: new recruit, mentor, team leader, and manager for a product unit in the functional area. Compensation is tied to the position on the ladder. There is a base wage that is below the industry average, plus a biennial bonus of up to 15 percent plus stock options and payroll deductions for stock purchases. Overtime is not paid.

## Intimate service: McKinsey

McKinsey provides a high quality of service. Projects usually have a long duration (from months to years), and the interaction with customers is important. McKinsey recruits top students from the best undergraduate and MBA programs. Preference is given to candidates with a technical background such as engineering and computer science, and who already have in-depth knowledge of a functional business area.

Training is extensive. In the UK, for example, training for the first year is completed on and off the job, in and out of the company, on technical skills and communications skills. On-the-job training consists of:

- Coaching – Managers are trained to develop the people with whom they work.

- Study experience – Consultants rotate through industries, clients, and types of business to ensure the broadest experience and build new skills.

- Mentoring – Each consultant has a mentor or a development leader. This is a senior consultant who monitors progress at the end of each study, gives feedback twice a year, and dispenses career advice.

- Off-the-job training consists of:
  - Language lessons. Recruits may take a four-week main business language course before joining McKinsey or, once hired, avail themselves of weekly in-office language training.
  - A three-week course on basic sets of skills (such as financial analysis and communication) and McKinsey functioning, run by the office consultants as well as external experts.
  - In-office training days on specific matters.
  - A worldwide McKinsey two-week course on consulting.

- There is also an in-house 'mini-MBA', a three-week crash course on financial and management skills for highly educated people.

Motivation is based on the potential career path inside the company (from consultant to partner) and the knowledge that McKinsey opens doors to management positions outside the company. The career path is based on the track record, progressing up a ladder to the highest position, senior partner. For fast-track people, it is possible to become a partner after five to six years of joining as an associate. Compensation is exceptional and evolves according to the career path.

# In any industry, people profiles vary with service level

All people strategies mentioned above can be seen within a single industry. Consider the following examples – four restaurants with different service strategies and correspondingly different approaches to human resources management.

# Service factory: McDonalds

Although the level of service quality is the same all over the world, customers generally do not stay long and need little advice. Nevertheless, to provide always and everywhere the same level of quality implies a specific type of human resource management and the use of specific levers.

Generally, McDonald's hires young people. Most of the employees are students and other young people working for the first time. The company's expertise lies in standardizing the know-how involved in the work and infusing every restaurant with the standardized procedures. Staff are taught the basics of work and discipline. Every new employee begins as a trainee on the easiest of jobs – cooking French fries – following the standardized procedures such as, for example, cooking times. Once that role is perfected, an employee moves to the next station and from there to another. Career prospects depend on the initiative shown by workers on the job. They may be offered opportunities for quick advancement, working their way to crew chief, then manager, and eventually to a position in corporate headquarters. Promotion is mostly given from within on the basis of skills and negotiating ability. Compensation is in general lower than in any other non-agricultural industry. It consists of a base wage plus a profit-sharing element. In the USA, there is the opportunity to buy stock in the company.

On the other hand, McDonald's takes care of its employees, offering a lot of fringe benefits and support. Some examples in the USA include:

▪ Health insurance for the 15,000 full-time employees.

▪ A network of hospitals across the USA that provides quality care and a discount to McDonald's employees who need medical care.

▪ Educational assistance program. Eligible employees (store management and assistants with at least six months of service) will be reimbursed for 75 percent of their course fees to a maximum of $400 per course.

▪ Sabbatical. After 10 years of service, employees are eligible for sabbatical leave.

▪ Child care.

In some countries, McDonald's provides services that are not readily available in the domestic market.

Levels of empowerment for customer recovery are specified carefully. If the hamburger or juice falls on the floor it is replaced, and there is a special key on the cash register to allow for it.

## Service chain: Disney

In theme restaurants, customers stay longer but generally need little advice. Again, very specific human resources tools are used with employees who deliver the service. Recruitment is based on relationship and communication skills. At the second interview, for example, three candidates are interviewed together for 45 minutes. This allows the interviewer to evaluate applicants closely by observing how each interacts with the others.

Once employees are recruited, they go through intensive training, longer than at McDonald's. There is training on technical aspects of the job as well as on company culture, know-how, and procedures. Training for the newly hired consists of:

- A two-day orientation seminar called 'Traditions' at Disney University. The aim is to provide employees, called cast members, with an understanding of Disney's corporate tradition and values and provide skills essential to job performance.
- Learning experiences at on-site practice sessions and classes at the university.
- Paired training, allowing exceptional cast members to act as role models for others.

The new cast members work with such a model. They are required to complete 16–48 hours of paired training, and are not allowed to interact with customers (called guests) until they successfully finish this, and answer questions on a training checklist. Training doesn't stop there. It is a continuous process. Depending on their function within the company, various courses are offered. For example, salaried cast members can attend classes on counseling and listening and understanding people as individuals. Disney also runs courses on courtesy, stress and time management, and other specific skills.

Motivation is important, because many of Disney's jobs are routine. Motivation is achieved by constantly praising cast members, as well as by having a communication and social relations program. There are service recognition parties and milestone banquets for 10, 15, and 20 years of service. And, annually, outstanding cast members are assigned a year at the Disney University. Another form of recognition is carried out during Christmas holidays. All Disney theme parks re-open on a particular evening for cast members and their families. The management, dressed in costumes, wishes them a happy holiday while operating the park.

Promotion is usually from within. Cast members who have managerial potential go through six months of on-the-job training. (This does not in itself guarantee that they will be promoted.)

## Personalized service: Harry's Bar

Typically, a bar is a place where the customer doesn't stay very long, but establishes a rapport with the barman. Recruitment is an important lever as the strength of interaction is high. The future barman has to respond to different criteria: to be extrovert, lively, and to be good at creating atmosphere. A knowledge of different languages is a top priority. Candidates are also tested on their technical knowledge, for example how to mix a specific cocktail. Generally, the recruits will have previous experience in a well-known bar with very good references. So Harry's Bar differs to McDonald's or Disney because it hires people who are already experts. Training is on the job. For the first two or three weeks, depending on the candidate, a barman will have no contact with customers. The recruit works in the bar, observing how the department manager reacts with the customers and watching and listening to conversations. After this period, the new barman will be allowed direct contact with customers. Other training includes technical aspects such as security.

Motivation is provided by high pay and such material incentives as cheap flight tickets after one year in the company, job opportunities within the group, and the reputation of Harry's Bar, which opens doors to other companies. There is also an employee of the month scheme.

Career prospects are based on a promotion ladder and on opportunities. Each career path is defined according to the knowledge candidates must have, and compensation is tied to the ladder. A typical career path is: barman, first barman, and service manager. The barman prepares cocktails and beverages. The first barman is responsible for the bar. The service manager is responsible for the whole unit, including sales and promotion. In Harry's Bar, the barman can also move from one department to another depending on the opportunities available and on his wishes. Generally, there are a lot of opportunities outside. There is constant personnel rotation in the hotel industry.

## Intimate service: a three star restaurant

A restaurant which has been awarded three Michelin stars – a sign that it is among the best in the world – will provide a service in which interaction is important, and contact between staff and customers lasts for some time. In fact, waiters give quite a lot of advice: which wines to choose for the dish, explanations about how different ingredients were cooked, and other culinary suggestions. People generally take their time to consider the menu. This is a high level of service with its own human resource levers.

Waiters who come into direct contact with customers are recruited by the head waiter, and are chosen from the best hospitality schools or on the basis of previous experience in another well-known restaurant which has given a very good reference. Presentation is important. Motivation and flexibility are the most essential recruitment criteria. The restaurant will give each new waiter a job specification booklet. This sets out the main tasks that are involved in the job, as well as the company culture and its rules of behavior. Training is on the job and is extensive. Each waiter is watched closely by a superior when working, and errors are corrected immediately. The recruit will be taught the technical aspects of the job (for example, how to cut the different meats) as well as the finer points and the house's practices. Each waiter can take on more and more responsibility. This means learning more and more tasks and perfecting them. The position a waiter occupies on the ladder and its related compensation will depend on the skills acquired. The career ladder is: steward, half-manager rank, rank manager, headwaiter assistant, first headwaiter, second headwaiter, and room manager. Generally, an employee stands a good chance of being hired at a higher level when applying for a job in another restaurant.

In a three-star restaurant, employees who leave to get experience in another restaurant may return later. Also, to motivate waiters, the restaurant will teach them to do as many different tasks as possible. People rotate on tasks, serving customers as well as setting the tables or attending to telephone reservations. When hiring, the company takes new recruits in hand. In fact, the headwaiter goes so far as to organize accommodation and insurance as well as administration procedures for those coming from abroad.

Compensation is linked to the individual's ability plus tips, which are shared among employees according to position. Wages are above the industry average. Also there are other fringe benefits that are difficult to find in the hospitality industry: three weeks' holiday during school summer holidays, two during school winter holidays, a third day holiday at Easter and Pentecost. There are Sunday and Mondays free and no work during Christmas.

As for customer service, the waiter is fully empowered. No referral to a higher authority is needed; the waiter's discretion covers everything from changing the wine, the dish, to substituting, to adding a chair or changing seating.

# Different departments need different people management

A service company is usually made up of different departments, with distinct human resources management needs. Figure 7.4 shows this in operation at a retail bank. It is obvious that, in each category, selection, training, development, empowerment, motivation, and support will be carried out in different ways. The same goes for the IT business, where maintenance requirements are different to those in development support. In many cases human resources policies must be tailored to the level of service provided by individual departments. As well as the way you have to treat different segments (as described in Chapter 1), one must move from thinking of different segments of people to tailoring your business policies to match the needs of individual customer segments. Even when considering employees within a single firm, you must move from thinking about 'personnel' to considering different segments of people, and then consider each individual. The key to treating each individual differently is the changing role of the manager.

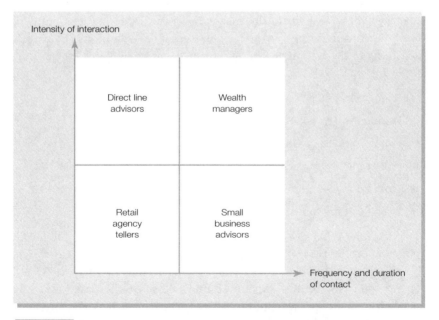

**Figure 7.4** Customer interactions vary from department to department in a retail bank

| Coaching | → | Skills |
|---|---|---|
| Training | → | Energy and communication |
| Tutoring | → | Making one's knowledge explicit for passing on |
| Mentoring | → | Having a network |
| Counseling | → | Asking questions |
| Evaluating | → | Observation and fairness |
| Inspiring | → | Creating vivid pictures of the future |

**Figure 7.5** The manager as a coach

# The manager's new role: as coach

Irrespective of which service industry you are in, or which part of the company you run, or what type of people you manage, your role as a manager will have dramatically changed over the last few years. Caring for customers means caring for your people – even if the definition of care varies according to the type of employee. The manager's role has changed in the following ways:

- From saying no to saying, yes – go ahead.
- From telling to asking.
- From saying to involving.
- From ordering to persuading.
- From knowing to letting others know.
- From deciding to inspiring.

The new role is that of a coach who prepares the team to perform to its full potential on the field. Once the action starts, the coach sits on the bench, helping players recuperate when tired, remotivating during breaks, and giving some advice and support. I have classified this role under six headings. This gives a sense of the skills required for each role (Figure 7.5).

## Training

In a service company, everyone must become a trainer – i.e., share knowledge and skills with other people. This is the only way to get more professional staff, motivate them, and give them opportunities for personal development. Some skills are needed to make your own knowledge explicit and transmittable. Good two-way communication and presentation abilities as well as pedagogical talents are necessary. A manager who knows how to be a teacher has the complete respect of the team when sharing know-how. At Taco Bell the CEO taught every induction training course from 1981 to 1995, explaining the philosophy and know-how as the company grew to 20,000 restaurants from high street to shopping malls to company and school cafeterias.

Managers are usually bad at training. They subcontract it too much outside the company. They don't attend the sessions, thus failing to signal that investing in people is important. If they attend, they make a speech but are afraid to teach. As a result they don't know their team or company staff's skill levels. They then expect too much; since they are incapable of transmitting knowledge, they get frustrated, as does the team. When theme restaurant chain Hippopotamus set up a quality program, the CEO came every week for six months to introduce or close the five-day training sessions.

## Tutoring

Training involves communicating knowledge to a 'class' or group of people, standing in front of the group, and employing a mix of techniques: presentations, cases, role plays, critical incidents, discussions. Tutoring, on the other hand, is a one-to-one transmission of know-how and skills. You start by assessing each of your team members individually. What is their present level of knowledge? What can they do today? To instill new skills or reinforce and improve existing ones you observe individuals and carry out 'mini-sessions' either as part of a schedule or at critical times (after a mistake is made or when confronted with a new situation). To be a good tutor requires patience and good individual follow-up abilities, as well as observation, communication, and demonstration skills. Tutoring methods are different to those used in training. Essentially there are three approaches:

1  Tell, then have the person tell.

2  Do, then have the person do.

3  Show, then have the person show.

Of course, a mix of all three may be used. It takes time. For the same body of knowledge, a training session will take a third or even a fifth of the time that a tutoring project takes. But tutoring is geared much more to the individual who needs particular help at a particular time than classroom training could ever be.

## Mentoring

Mentoring involves helping the team and its members make best use of the organization to do the job properly. It means spelling out the rules of the game, in-house style, orienting people towards other units, department or individuals who might help them do their job, or grow their job. It supports the team by providing the necessary organizational environment. You can even protect the team from all the hassles of procedures, policies, and interfaces by providing a buffer (possibly yourself) between them and pressures from elsewhere in the organization. This role requires knowledge about the organization, administrative skills, and the ability to help, convince or even convert when people do not understand the 'stupid rules.' The manager is the person explaining why we do it in a certain way, and is frank to people who do not play by the established rules. As a mentor, you spread the word. Living by the company values, you set an example; you help project values. If one views the corporation's ethos as two concentric circles, an inner circle and an outer one, the role of the mentor becomes clearer. Mentoring is involved in promoting the inner circle, which represents core values – the core ways of doing things that have made the company a success – and defining the boundaries of autonomy – that is, where trespassing is not permissible. The more space between the two circles, the more autonomy there will be for the people mentored.

## Counseling

Counseling helps team members solve problems. I often say that there are two key questions a manager should ask his or her team every day:

- 'How are you today?' (Caring for the others.)
- 'How can I help you today?'(Showing concern for and commitment to the inverted pyramid, in which the manager's role is to serve those who serve customers.)

Counseling helps define objectives and problems (that is, gaps between what is and what should be). It helps define options, steps towards solutions, and responsibilities in execution. Counseling requires listening skills, and an ability to reformulate, evaluate, and provide creative ideas and alternative choices. It requires the ability to help people focus on key issues, ensuring that commitments needed to make things happen are well spelled out. As counselor, the manager becomes a resource that is used at the discretion of his or her team members. If they don't ask for help, they don't need it!

## Evaluating

Give feedback on good as well as sub-standard performance. Annual reviews make no sense unless constant feedback is given – that is, unless they are specific, fast and to the point. Not only does evaluation help motivate staff to continue doing well, it identifies areas where improvements can be made. Whereas compliments can be made publicly, reprimands should be handed out in private. You can judge a service organization's approach to its people very quickly by observing how often compliments are paid, and whether public settings are used when giving negative feedback. The worst case is when no feedback at all is given, or when only negative feedback is provided. The second worst outcome – and this happens in many organizations – is a lack of follow-up, or a lack of courtesy and appreciation upon seeing improvements. Finally, the third worst scenario is accepting sub-standard work from some people for too long: This discourages all other members of a team from doing well. Critical competencies here are observation, fact finding, communication skills, sincerity, and follow-up.

## Inspiring

This means creating vivid pictures of the future, providing learning and development opportunities at each contact, and giving meaning to what the team is doing by frequently returning to the reasons why things are done. Everybody is immersed in day-to-day activities. When pedaling a bicycle, it is difficult to see yourself cycling! From time to time, everybody needs someone else's vision, explanations, and orientations to help them refocus, understand what they do, and find better and more effective ways of doing it. This is achieved by refocusing on objectives. Creating such pictures requires enthusiasm, imagination, the ability to describe what does not exist in concrete terms, and communication skills to explain and re-explain the reasons why. Unfortunately, as managers, we are impelled to provide inputs more about what to do and how to do it rather than why. This may help in the short term, but staff fail to develop; employees are left merely executing what they have been told to do. In the event of a new or unprecedented situation (often in front of the customers), the rules governing what to do and how to behave no longer suffice. Although these policies may have worked in the past, and have now hardened into a procedure, it prevents people from thinking on their feet and acting differently in response to a new situation.

Consider the following. Recently I arrived at an airport gate to check in at 7:00 a.m. for a European flight that was scheduled to depart at 7:30. The hostess ticked me off for not being there at the specified time, which was 35 minutes before departure. I asked whether the plane was full, and whether there was still any room. She said that the problem was with the breakfast tray. I offered to pass on breakfast since I was late. The response: 'The rule is that if you don't have a tray, you don't get in the plane.' The passenger had become an appendix to a tray! Why? One supposes that a catering subcontractor charges the airline for unused trays. The trays would have been ordered by counting the names on the list of passengers on the computer. To reduce costs, a manager has set up a process whereby the gate hostess calls passengers 30 minutes before departure, telling the subcontractor the exact number of trays required, thus eliminating waste. But the priorities were inverted: no tray, no passenger. That is how people can lose sight of the bigger picture. In this instance, the hostess was not to blame. At fault was the boss who failed to explain the rationale.

## Sustaining a service culture: mindset changes

A culture is based on shared values. How do we view customers, how do we view the roles of our teams, how do we view the link between customer orientation and economic performance? Those shared values must be translated into behavior to be effective. How do we behave when faced with a customer problem? How do we react in front of a dilemma: protecting the interest of a customer at an extra cost to ourselves? How much time do we spend on customer issues versus other business issues? And so on.

These issues are easy to tackle when a company is relatively small. But they require a more conscious effort when a company has grown in size, and/or has lost its customer orientation because of success. Many companies have reached a stage where they require mindset changes.

When Virgin Atlantic Airways started, Richard Branson was aboard almost every flight, welcoming passengers and crew alike. As the company grew, he remained in contact with customers for inaugural flights, continuing to get involved in events when introducing innovations, new routes or new products to defend the consumer against the dinosaur (i.e. British Airways). As far as employees were concerned, he invited them to see him at regular meetings, and maintained an open-door policy.

However, as a company grows, it becomes more difficult for its founder/CEO/entrepreneur to continue personally to reinforce a culture he created. Can this personal involvement be replaced by a system or a process? Can a service culture be institutionalized in such a way that it can go on forever? If yes, what are the ingredients/factors that will contribute to such institutionalization?

I have identified a few factors that I think might contribute to this. Some are hard factors, some are softer ones.

## Mindset

Mindset has to do with the right attitudes and behavior in terms of how much we value the customers, the teams, customer service. Mindset is usually developed in induction training (for new employees) and enforced through different devices such as spending a day in the shoes of the customer, or in another department within the organization in order to better understand the other's viewpoint.

## Mindset reinforcement

Mindset can be reinforced through key performance indicators that emphasize how well a company has attracted, satisfied and retained its customers. If customer satisfaction is key, then a substantial part of the manager's bonus should be linked to customer satisfaction. In other words, the key performance indicators must be linked to the incentive system.

## Mindset mapping

In order to develop a certain mindset, you need a proper representation (a map) of what you want people to have in mind, i.e. what it is that you are trying to convey. As organizations get bigger, what could once be spoken has to be formalized (written, documented, printed, photographed, filmed, etc.) so that it can be used as a storyboard for everyone, and especially used in induction seminars. Nike went without writing down its values until 1992 (almost 20 years after its creation), by which time it had more than 4,000 employees.

## Mindset exchange

Mindset exchange has to do with the way best practices are communicated and live a life of their own without the boss having constantly to repeat what is important and less important: best practice sharing, celebrations of positive behavior, publishing extraordinary stories in in-house magazines, and publishing the results of surveys and results of qualitative research. All these things contribute to mindset exchange.

## Mindset duplication

How do you get all employees thinking on the same wavelength as staff in, say, another country? Internal promotion, mobility, and cross-skilling can do a lot to duplicate and institutionalize a particular mindset. At Photo Service, a one-hour photo processing lab, the technicians who develop the prints also know how to welcome customers and sell them films and accessories. There is no difference between customer facing and behind the scenes staff. Cross-skilling like this not only allows better management of in-store traffic; it also allows everyone to be in contact with customers, not just sales staff.

At Carrefour, when a branch is opened in a new country, the company doesn't hire local managers to begin with. It sends seasoned Carrefour staff to the new country. They set up shop, make sure the company ethos is nurtured and kept intact, and only after opening do they transfer the day-to-day running of the store to local managers.

## Mindset cherishing

All staff need to feel not just that they belong to the company, but that the company belongs to them. This can be done in two ways. One is to replace large organizational structures with smaller units, led by entrepreneurs or 'intrapreneurs.' This is what we did at Disneyland Paris. We eradicated a centralized, hierarchical structure that was too inflexible to respond or adapt to customer needs. A team of 12,000 people and nine layers was slimmed down to 250 'small worlds' of 50 cast members. Only three layers of hierarchy remained as a result of this.

The second way is to spread ownership of the company via whatever mechanism is most suitable, to the largest number of people. Starbucks has managed this. Everyone is a shareholder.

## Mindset leadership

Last but not least, how should the Phil Knights (Nike's founder) and the Richard Bransons of this world be replaced? How can we select and nurture the 'torch bearers' of a company who will continue to promote successfully the values and ethos of a company? Should it be a COO (chief operating officer) or someone else promoted from within the management team? No matter what organizational arrangement is made, the torchbearers need to spend enough time with the entrepreneur/founder/initial CEO to share their values, and take the torch from there.

# A new language, a new dictionary to reinforce the culture

'The verb precedes action,' said Goethe. Whereas words can mean nothing if not followed by commitment, they can do a lot if they are used to precede commitment. We need to rewrite the vocabulary we use to express what we mean, to express a true commitment toward whatever we do. If customer service or customer orientation are what we think is necessary to get great performance, then the wording of all internal communications should express it. The same goes with what we express externally.

Where are we using words that might indicate that we are not totally committed to what we say? In plenty of places: from banners, to posters, to titles, functions, and names of places. I shall not consider the documentation, letters, e-mail, faxes, and contracts received by customers in this chapter. This section focuses on how staff should speak differently about what they do for their teams and customers. I shall illustrate the need to revisit our vocabulary for better reinforcement of a customer orientation: functions, titles, and job descriptions; talking about customers; talking about employees and places.

## Functions, titles, and job descriptions: where is the customer?

'Your job is to protect the merchandise.' This was the first sentence written in the job description of sales people of one of the biggest European department stores I was invited to help. Yes, there are people who steal in shops. But to display an attitude of merchandise protection is not going to facilitate positive interactions for the vast majority of customers who don't!

What does your contact person's job description say? Does it mention what they do for the company or what they do for the customers? 'I am the head of marketing,' 'I am a salesman,' great! Except that marketing means doing something to the market, and salesman means selling, not necessarily helping the customer buy! How about Head of Customer Relations instead, or Product Advisor, or Solution Provider, or Customer Support Manager?

What do your key job titles say about you? Can't you change them to demonstrate customer orientation? To go even further, renaming certain functions make a difference: should it be 'headquarters' or 'central services'? Should it be 'supply chain and logistics' or 'demand chain and delivery support'?

A little creativity coupled with a true attempt to show service orientation in job description, titles, and functions is a good way to reinforce the culture. At Disney, you do not have customers and employees but guests and cast members – what a wonderful way to say that the role of the employees is to welcome and take care of the guests, and that all employees play a role, with the corresponding costume. At GrandVision, we wrote senior job descriptions as poems. And, of course, each poem describes the way each of these senior executives, including the CEO, contributes to their teams and the rest of the organization!

## Everyday language: Does it reflect customer orientation?

Do we sell or do we help customers buy? Do we cross or up-sell or do we help customers buy more? Or do we offer peace of mind by providing the right level of assistance? Do we have a more meaningful name for customers than 'accounts'? Do we use staff or employees or 'team members' or 'associates' (like Starbucks)? Do we write 'no entry' on a door (negative) or 'exit only' (positive)? (Disney). Do we answer letters of complaint in technical jargon or make it easy for the customer to understand our response? (Cellphone operators and their 'roaming' charges are a classic example of something nobody can understand.) How about our commercial proposals, documentation, and contracts? Do they highlight what is important for the customer to know before signing, or is it hidden in footnotes? Even when we use satisfaction surveys, do we use the word 'questionnaire' (I am questioning you!) or 'feedback' – e.g., your 'eyes and ears' please (Disney), or 'sweet or sour, tell us please' (Châteauform). Do we describe our products in terms of features, or in terms of benefits to the customers?

Try to list in your company the most common words you use to describe customers, their behavior, your own behavior, and what you do to them (rather than with them). The same with employees: titles, functions etc. Reread your documentation, and for each existing word or expression find a synonym. This can greatly help in reinforcing customer commitment. Also try to list your most frequently asked questions and find alternative ways to express them to demonstrate your customer commitment. For instance, when a subordinate calls you, do you always ask 'What is it' (or something similar) or 'How can I help you?' (or something similar)?

# Creating trust within a company: a discipline!

Trust is part of the company culture. Trust allows empowerment and decentralization of decision making to those who are close to the customer. In turn, it leads to better serving of customer needs by fast problem solving and appropriate recovery. It helps create the brand, and thus sales and profit. Trust is not a one-way street: In order for the team to trust the leader, the leader must trust the team! Nor is it instantaneous. It takes time to build trust but no time to lose it! It takes time because one member of the team must feel comfortable about the other. This trust means that whatever the other is doing or saying, it is taken at face value without questioning for a hidden agenda. And the level of trust increases when consistency of behavior is observed in the other to the point where one can say: 'I can predict what he would say or do in such circumstances.' No single situation can lead to such predictability. It is the repetition of consistent behavior across different situations and locations that leads someone to say: 'That person is predictable and I can trust him or her.'

Trust is not just about predictability, it is also about respect. Respect for the ability of the other to perform, for the quality of his or her judgment. Lack of respect leads to seeing flaws in the other's words or actions. In turn this leads to lack of cooperation or delegation.

Trust is not free of charge. It is an investment in a relationship. I can trust someone when I know them well. But it can be destroyed very fast: simply if a decision is taken without enough explanation. An e-mail – short and precise, but without the non-verbal contact – can destroy it as quickly.

Trust leads to empowerment at all levels of the organization, which in turn leads to more responsiveness toward customers. Companies with low trust from the top towards the teams, from the managers to their subordinates, cannot develop a fully-fledged customer service orientation.

# Creating incentives based on customer success

If culture is not just about values (i.e. what we believe in) but also about resulting behavior (i.e. what we do), incentives can reinforce culture.

To make the new mindset effective at Disneyland Paris, within the new structure of 250 small worlds, performance and bonuses were assessed on three equally weighted factors for each small world: customer satisfaction, cast member satisfaction, and economic result (cost, revenue or profit).

When Xerox embarked on its leadership quality program it introduced a team bonus at district level: The sales manager, delivery manager and after-sale manager jointly got their bonuses based on customer satisfaction. At the most basic level, for a homogeneous business, customer satisfaction could serve as a basis for attributing bonus or part of the remuneration. A rule of thumb says that at least half of the total incentive should be based on this objective. This easy measure can be used for a single business or for multiple businesses within the same corporation.

At a more advanced level, i.e. when wanting to differentiate between functions (production/finance/marketing/after sales), then additional criteria can be used:

- Internal client satisfaction.
- Customer growth or share for sales people serving large accounts – but also customer retention over time.
- Team based satisfaction for sales, delivery, and after sales, as in the case of Xerox.

No matter what criteria are used, what is key is that the incentive given should reflect the importance given to service and to customers. Then the actual benefit can be in the form of bonus, stock option, promotion, or whatever the company deems suitable.

# Summary

In conclusion, this chapter has concentrated on three people-management issues that can foster good service.

1 Adapting human resources policies to the requirements of the type of service provided.

**2** The specific role of the manager as a coach. All studies show that good people management leads not only to good service but also to better productivity.

**3** Developing means to sustain a service-oriented culture. This has to do with mindset, language, and incentives.

Here is how a retail group has spelled out the 10 rights and obligations of its staff:

# Our associates' rights

**1** The right to do everything necessary to satisfy each customer.

**2** The right to take the initiative and try new things.

**3** The right to provide constructive criticism.

**4** The right to make a mistake.

**5** The right to understand.

**6** The right to be trained.

**7** The right to a working environment that one is proud of.

**8** The right to be recognized for one's achievements.

**9** The right to develop at one's own pace within the company.

**10** The right to help and support.

# Our associates' responsibilities

**1** The responsibility to do everything possible to satisfy each customer.

**2** The responsibility to be a team player and contribute to the team's performance.

**3** The responsibility to be a trainer and mentor.

**4** The responsibility to share.

**5** The responsibility to lead by example.

**6** The responsibility to be honest and loyal.

**7** The responsibility to respect one's commitments and those of the company.

8   The responsibility to be accountable for one's actions.

9   The responsibility to have new ideas.

10   The responsibility to constantly improve.

## Don'ts

1   Don't underinvest in people. Recruitment time for a steward or hostess at Singapore Airlines is nine hours. How much time does your company spend?

2   Don't treat your people differently to how you want them to treat your customers.

3   Don't benchmark human resources practice against the wrong service type.

4   Don't expect your people to serve customers if you don't serve your people.

5   Don't expect autonomy if you have not developed autonomous people.

6   Don't create too many rules without having mechanisms in place for breaking them from time to time.

7   Don't stifle initiative by leaving too little room for empowerment.

8   Don't use a language that is not customer oriented.

## The 10 people questions

You must adapt your HR policies to your service requirements, and your managers must be good coaches.

1   Do they spend time in the classroom – as teachers?

2   Do they spend time explaining the reasons why, rather than merely stating what's to be done and how?

3   Do they know how to help others solve problems?

4   Do they represent the company values as torchbearers?

5   Do they break the rules if they consider them stupid?

6   Do they know how to whistleblow if someone is breaking the rules?

7   Do they provide regular feedback?

8   Do they know how to paint a vivid picture of the future?

9   Is your language customer oriented?

10  Are at least 50 percent of your incentives related to customer satisfaction?

# Conclusion

Dear Reader,

In conclusion, I would like to invite you to make your own plan for action. To help you focus on key issues, I have developed a self-assessment tool, included over the next few pages. It is divided into 10 sections, each pertaining to one aspect of customer service and customer orientation. If you need more questionnaires to get your company's feedback, please feel free to send me an e-mail (*horovitz@imd.ch*) and I will happily send an electronic copy.

I hope you have enjoyed reading this book. I will be happy if you have got one very big idea and five small ideas from it to improve your business.

Regards,

Jacques Horovitz

# Mobilizing the organization for superior customer orientation

The purpose of this short questionnaire is for you to assess to what extent your organization has created and developed a service culture. The questions cover seven main areas of service culture development: Developing a customer philosophy; Setting the example as a manager; Empowering and involving; Linking incentives to customer orientation; Communicating and celebrating the customer culture; Focusing measurements on customer orientation; Following up on improvements.

Complete your answers, score yourself on each section, and then complete the spider chart on the final page.

# Step 1   Answer the questions below

## 1. Develop a customer philosophy

| Statement<br><br>Read each statement and then decide to what extent you believe it applies to the company where you work.<br><br>At my company... | Strongly agree<br><br>Score 5 | Agree<br><br>Score 4 | Neither agree or disagree<br><br>Score 3 | Disagree<br><br>Score 2 | Strongly disagree<br><br>Score 1 |
|---|---|---|---|---|---|
| Fulfilling customer needs drives the strategy of the company | | | | | |
| Staff consider that the customer is always right | | | | | |
| We have a widely communicated service concept with defined levels of excellence | | | | | |
| We treat customer complaints very seriously, and endeavor to resolve them in the shortest possible time | | | | | |
| We actively encourage feedback and suggestions from the customer | | | | | |
| We regularly send staff to experience the customer's views | | | | | |
| Our current customers are treated as more important than potential new customers | | | | | |
| We continually update our understanding of what our customers expect from us | | | | | |
| We have a 'can do' attitude with respect to serving our customers | | | | | |
| We recognize that even our internal departments have customers to satisfy | | | | | |

Develop a customer philosophy

Total score

## 2. Set the example as a manager

| Statement<br><br>Read each statement and then decide to what extent you believe it applies to the company where you work.<br><br>At my company … | Strongly agree<br><br>Score 5 | Agree<br><br>Score 4 | Neither agree or disagree<br><br>Score 3 | Disagree<br><br>Score 2 | Strongly disagree<br><br>Score 1 |
|---|---|---|---|---|---|
| **Managers always talk about the customer respectfully in front of employees** | | | | | |
| **Managers give employees the same respect with which they expect employees to treat customers** | | | | | |
| **Managers are obsessed with customer satisfaction, and take real pride in commitment to the customer** | | | | | |
| **In our managers' offices, we can see with our own eyes that the commitment to the customers is there (banners, signs, etc.)** | | | | | |
| **One of the key roles of the manager is to teach and encourage their staff to serve the customer better** | | | | | |
| **Managers are role models for excellent customer service** | | | | | |
| **Managers see customer satisfaction as more important than financial results** | | | | | |
| **Managers always explain to the front line staff in direct contact with the customers why certain procedures exist** | | | | | |
| **Managers see their role as helping the front line staff to serve the customer better** | | | | | |
| **Managers never ask for their own needs to be prioritized while the customer is being served** | | | | | |

Total score

**Set the example as a manager**

## 3. Empower and involve

| Statement<br><br>Read each statement and then decide to what extent you believe it applies to the company where you work.<br><br>At my company … | Strongly agree<br><br>Score 5 | Agree<br><br>Score 4 | Neither agree or disagree<br><br>Score 3 | Disagree<br><br>Score 2 | Strongly disagree<br><br>Score 1 |
|---|---|---|---|---|---|
| We under-promise and over-deliver to the customer | | | | | |
| We are very good at collecting customer service improvement ideas from the front line staff who are in regular contact with the customer | | | | | |
| We regularly have projects and initiatives that aim to improve customer service | | | | | |
| Front line staff in regular contact with the customer are empowered to solve problems for customers as they arise | | | | | |
| Front line staff in regular touch with the customer have the freedom to try out new solutions for the customer | | | | | |
| We trust our front line staff to 'do the right thing' when serving the customer | | | | | |
| Front line staff have all the necessary tools they need to serve the customer to their best ability | | | | | |
| We hold front line staff accountable for their actions toward the customers | | | | | |
| We allow front line staff to commit mistakes as long as they are not repeated | | | | | |
| Front line staff receive comprehensive training in how to serve the customer | | | | | |

**Empower and involve**

Total
score

## 4. Link incentives to customer orientation

| Statement<br><br>Read each statement and then decide to what extent you believe it applies to the company where you work.<br><br>At my company … | Strongly agree<br><br>Score 5 | Agree<br><br>Score 4 | Neither agree or disagree<br><br>Score 3 | Disagree<br><br>Score 2 | Strongly disagree<br><br>Score 1 |
|---|---|---|---|---|---|
| We understand the key elements that contribute to customer satisfaction | | | | | |
| We link compensation of front line employees in regular contact with the customer to customer satisfaction | | | | | |
| Customer orientation is an important factor when promoting managers | | | | | |
| We recognize people who give exceptional service to the customer | | | | | |
| We reward people who give exceptional service to the customer (prizes, bonus, etc.) | | | | | |
| We have team incentives where teamwork is important to serve the customer | | | | | |
| New ideas for improving customer service are recognized and celebrated | | | | | |
| We circulate true stories within our company of exceptional customer service | | | | | |
| We publicly acknowledge letters of compliments from customers (display letters, publish letters in company magazines, read letters at staff meetings, etc.) | | | | | |
| Front line staff who give excellent customer service are treated as company icons | | | | | |

Link incentives to customer orientation

Total
score

## 5. Communicate and celebrate the customer culture

**Statement**

Read each statement and then decide to what extent you believe it applies to the company where you work.

**At my company ...**

| | Strongly agree | Agree | Neither agree or disagree | Disagree | Strongly disagree |
|---|---|---|---|---|---|
| | Score 5 | Score 4 | Score 3 | Score 2 | Score 1 |
| Results of customer satisfaction surveys are widely distributed | | | | | |
| The key elements of customer satisfaction are widely known | | | | | |
| Customers are encouraged to visit and discuss their level of satisfaction with our products and services | | | | | |
| Issues related to customers have a high profile in management meetings | | | | | |
| Customer information is shared within and between departments and functions | | | | | |
| Feedback from the customer is widely shared and discussed | | | | | |
| New staff induction programs devote substantial time to explaining the needs and expectations of the customers | | | | | |
| We are proud of the way in which we handle customer complaints | | | | | |
| Senior management emphasize their commitment to excellent customer service at all possible opportunities | | | | | |
| We use feedback from customers to improve our customer service | | | | | |

**Communicate and celebrate customer culture**

**Total score**

## 6. Focus measurements on customer orientation

**Statement**

Read each statement and then decide to what extent you believe it applies to the company where you work.

**At my company ...**

| | Strongly agree | Agree | Neither agree or disagree | Disagree | Strongly disagree |
|---|---|---|---|---|---|
| | Score 5 | Score 4 | Score 3 | Score 2 | Score 1 |
| We regularly measure customer satisfaction | | | | | |
| Customer satisfaction measurements are regarded as highly important | | | | | |
| Our customer satisfaction survey gives enough detail to allow meaningful actions to be taken | | | | | |
| The results of our customer satisfaction survey are presented in a motivating way | | | | | |
| We ask customers who stop buying from us why that is | | | | | |
| We benchmark our customer satisfaction surveys against other companies | | | | | |
| We measure the number of customer complaints that we receive | | | | | |
| We measure customer loyalty | | | | | |
| We measure the customer satisfaction generated by our departments for internal customers | | | | | |
| We regularly measure employee satisfaction | | | | | |

Focus measurements on customer orientation

Total score

## 7. Follow up on improvements

| Statement<br><br>Read each statement and then decide to what extent you believe it applies to the company where you work.<br><br>**At my company ...** | Strongly agree<br><br>Score 5 | Agree<br><br>Score 4 | Neither agree or disagree<br><br>Score 3 | Disagree<br><br>Score 2 | Strongly disagree<br><br>Score 1 |
|---|---|---|---|---|---|
| **We regularly invest in changes that will increase perceived value for the customer** | | | | | |
| **We regularly invest in changes that will reduce costs for the customer** | | | | | |
| **We clearly identify obstacles that are getting in the way of improving customer satisfaction** | | | | | |
| **We have clear and measurable goals for how we will increase customer satisfaction** | | | | | |
| **The goals that we have for improving customer service are ambitious** | | | | | |
| **Top management regularly reviews progress on customer satisfaction towards predetermined goals** | | | | | |
| **Managers are held accountable for increasing customer satisfaction** | | | | | |
| **Everyone knows their role in improving customer satisfaction** | | | | | |
| **If a major customer left the company then management would investigate why** | | | | | |
| **We exchange best practice on how to improve customer service** | | | | | |

Total score

**Follow up on improvements**

# Step 2  Summarize your results

Collect your results from each section of the questionnaire.

| Section | Results |
|---|---|
| 1   Develop a customer philosophy | |
| 2   Set the example as a manager | |
| 3   Empower and involve | |
| 4   Link incentives to customer orientation | |
| 5   Communicate and celebrate the customer culture | |
| 6   Focus measurements on customer orientation | |
| 7   Follow up on improvements | |

Now graph your results on the following page by marking off your results along each axis and then joining the points.

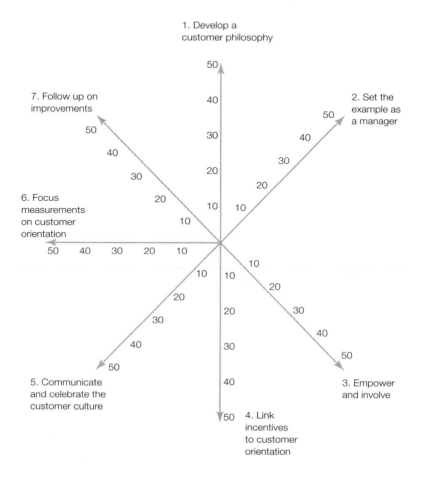

1. Develop a
customer philosophy

7. Follow up on
improvements

2. Set the
example as
a manager

6. Focus
measurements
on customer
orientation

5. Communicate
and celebrate the
customer culture

3. Empower
and involve

4. Link
incentives
to customer
orientation

# Index